About Laura

Laura Cole Gonzalez is the Transformational Author to the #1 best-seller **Healthy Business, Healthy You Toolbox** book series, **Action Attraction Planner™**, Speaker and Vision Board Coach.
She is the Founder of *Success School for Entrepreneurs* and the *Wellness Toolbox Club*.
She is a wife and mother to two sons.

Recognized as the go-to business development expert, Laura has a treasure trove of practical, highly effective tools to help you live your life, improve your health, and take your business success to the next level.

Laura has a holistic approach and a passion for wellness, digital marketing, and technology. Her 20+ years of experience as a Business Visionary and Marketing Mentor for the Natural Health and Wellness industry give entrepreneurs quick, easy, and practical access to life-changing techniques, transformational tools, and powerful healing processes.

She provides you with the knowledge and tools you need to eliminate struggle, overcome overwhelm, and build a solid foundation to thrive in your business and your health.

DISCLAIMER

The information in this book is for educational purposes only. All matters regarding physical and mental health should be supervised by a health practitioner knowledgeable in treating that particular condition. This book is not intended to provide medical, legal or financial advice or to take the place of medical, legal or financial advice and/or treatment from a qualified professional. Neither the author nor the publisher shall be liable or responsible for any loss, injury or damage allegedly arising for any information or suggestion in this book

www.LivewithLaura.com

Author Toolbox Publishing
Po Box 4429
Brick, NJ 08724

info@virtualbiz4u.com

Action Attraction ™ Planner

This planner was created as a complementary tool to the *Healthy Business, Healthy You Toolbox* Book and *30 Day Transformation Challenge* Online Programs to help you take action and focus to achieve your goals.

I developed this tool during one of the most challenging times of my life, and it turned into a universal tool that can be used in every aspect of life and business. This tool helped me overcome severe and debilitating health challenges, weight loss, and with my family, finances, business, and authorship. Every area of my life has benefitted from using this tool and it is my WISH that it will help you too.

Be sure to grab a copy of "**Healthy Business, Healthy You Toolbox**" book and take the 30 day Online Program to maximize the use of this Action Attraction ™ Planner. Book and Program is available at https://www.LivewithLaura.com

1 - **Wish, Feeling and Goal** pages – What is your Wish? What is your Goal to achieve the Wish? How does it Feel to achieve the Goal? Color in the Titles on Wish, Feeling and Goal "Adult Color Book" pages and is a Right Brain Creative activity. Trust me it will help you with your goals this month ☺

2 - Find and PIN on your Pinterest "**Virtual Vision Board**" the **photos** that will be printed and put on the Wish, Feeling and Goal pages. The photos will help you keep laser focused on your goal and also allow you to use your RAS (Reticular Activation System) in your brain to help you keep focused and achieve your goals.

3 - "**Sticky Notes**" This sheet is to get you planning so you can start using the Daily, Weekly and Monthly pages to plan out your Goal you want to achieve in the next 30 days. Place "sticky notes" on the sheets to help you stay laser focused on the milestone and tasks necessary to achieve your goal.

4 - **Action Attraction Plan** –includes a combination of goals, objectives, strategies and actions to provide your road map and path. This helps you to stay focused on the tasks necessary to achieve your goal.

5 - **Circle of 5 Support System** – Having a Circle of 5 in your life helps support you. Think of the group of supporters who will help you reach your dreams and goals.

6 - **Daily Planner** - Each day create your new Milestones and Action Step Tasks for that Day.

7 - **Weekly Planner** - Allows you to look at the week at a glance and plan accordingly.

8 - **Monthly Planner** – Gives you a 30 day road map to show you where you are going and what you want to achieve.

9 - **Meal Planner** – Nourishing Meal Planning will provide you to take better care of YOU, the most important asset in your life and business.

10 - **Monthly Money Budget** - Healthy wealth wisdom tool to help you take a pulse on your money budget and goals.

Photo Goes Here

WISH

Photo Goes Here

GOAL

Photo Goes Here

FEELING

Sticky Note Milestone	Sticky Note Task
Sticky Note Task	Sticky Note Task
Sticky Note Task	Sticky Note Task

________________ Day/Week

Provide online training for the YL team - schedule April - Aug to start

Write out my ideal client & their characteristics

Find 111 Tribe 111 People u want on our team & as future clients

Sticky Note Task

Sticky Note Task

Sticky Note Task

Sticky Note Task

________________ Day/Week

My Action Attraction Plan

Goal ______________________________

Milestones	Strategies	Action Steps

My Action Attraction Plan

Goal ____

Support/Resources	Target Date	Completion Date

Circle of 5 Support System

My Circle of 5 Support System

Friends	Health Team	Mentors	Influencers	Inspirational

My Monthly Planner

MONTH ______________________

Monday	Tuesday	Wednesday	Thursday

Healthy You Measurements			
Chest		Upper Arm	
Waist		Thigh	
Hips		Calf	

My Monthly Planner

MONTH ______________________

Friday	Saturday	Sunday	Special Notes

My Fitness Goals

Thank you!

Thank you for purchasing the **Action Attraction ™ Planner** and your support. It is much appreciated.

I want to give you several "Laura goodies" as THANK YOU Gifts for YOU.
Amazon doesn't let me know who purchases the planner so I want to make sure that I can thank you properly and also provide you additional support.

Please go here **https://livewithlaura.com/aapgifts**
and get your "Laura goodies" GIFTS – Tools that will help you while using the Action Attraction Planner.

THANK YOU Gift for YOU.

Make sure you also visit the back of the planner to also get your $200 off coupon code for access to the *30 Day Transformational challenge* for $97 (Value $297).

My Monthly Budget

MY INCOME	
Net Income 1 - Monthly	$
Net Income 2 - Monthly	$
Net Income 3 - Monthly	$
Other 1	$
Other 2	$

MY UTILITIES	
Cellular Phone	$
Electricity	$
Gas Utility	$
Heating Utility	$
Internet	$
Mortgage 2	$
Mortgage/Rent	$
Sewer Utility	$
Television/Cable	$
Trash Removal	$
Water	$
Other 1	$
Other 2	$

MY AUTO EXPENSES	
Auto Loan/Lease 1	$
Auto Loan/Lease 2	$
Auto Fuel	$
Auto Insurance	$
Auto Repairs	$
Commuting Expenses	$
Tolls	$
Other 1	$
Other 2	$

MY HOME EXPENSES	
Clothing	$
Credit Card 1	$
Credit Card 2	$
Food - Grocery	$
Food - Restaurant	$
Housekeeper	$
Shoes	$
Uniforms	$
Other 1	$
Other 2	$

My Healthy Money quote

MY HEALTH EXPENSES	
Gym Membership	$
Health Insurance	$
Medical	$
Oils/Suplements	$
Prescriptions	$
Vacation	$
Other 1	$
Other 2	$

MY FAMILY EXPENSES	
Baby Sitting	$
Child Care	$
Education	$
Entertainment	$
Presents/Gifts	$
Sports/Clubs	$
Tuition/Loans	$
Other 1	$
Other 2	$

MY MISCELLANEOUS EXPENSES	
Charitable Contributions	$
Income Taxes	$
Life Insurance 1	$
Life Insurance 2	$
Local Taxes	$
Real Estate Taxes	$
Retirement	$
Other 1	$
Other 2	$

My Money Goal

My Weekly Planner

My Categories	Monday __/__/__	Tuesday __/__/__	Wednesday __/__/__

My Weekly Planner

Thursday __/__/__	Friday __/__/__	Saturday __/__/__	Sunday __/__/__

My Meal Planner

For Week of / /

	Breakfast	Lunch	Dinner	Groceries
Monday				
Tuesday				
Wednesday				
Thursday				
Friday				
Saturday				
Sunday				

Special Instructions and Notes

My Daily Planner

My Schedule for __/__/__

6:00 AM	
7:00 AM	
8:00 AM	
9:00 AM	
10:00 AM	
11:00 AM	
12:00 PM	
1:00 PM	
2:00 PM	
3:00 PM	
4:00 PM	
5:00 PM	
6:00 PM	
7:00 PM	
8:00 PM	
9:00 PM	
10:00 PM	
11:00 PM	
12:00 AM	

Daily Affirmation / Prayer / Inspirational Quote	Hours Slept

Excercise	Time Spent	Water	Daily Goals
		○ ○ ○ ○	
		○ ○ ○ ○	
		○ ○ ○ ○	

Nutritional Journal

	Nourishing Meals	Supplements/Essential Oils
BRKFST		
LNCH		
DNR		

Greens ○ Beans ○ Onions ○ Mushroom ○ Berries ○ Seeds ○

My Daily Planner

My Schedule for ___/___/___

6:00 AM
7:00 AM
8:00 AM
9:00 AM
10:00 AM
11:00 AM
12:00 PM
1:00 PM
2:00 PM
3:00 PM
4:00 PM
5:00 PM
6:00 PM
7:00 PM
8:00 PM
9:00 PM
10:00 PM
11:00 PM
12:00 AM

Daily Affirmation / Prayer / Inspirational Quote	Hours Slept

Excercise	Time Spent	Water	Daily Goals
		O O O O	
		O O O O	
		O O O O	

Nutritional Journal		
	Nourishing Meals	Supplements/Essential Oils
BRKFST		
LNCH		
DNR		

Greens O Beans O Onions O Mushroom O Berries O Seeds O

My Daily Planner

My Schedule for __/__/__

6:00 AM
7:00 AM
8:00 AM
9:00 AM
10:00 AM
11:00 AM
12:00 PM
1:00 PM
2:00 PM
3:00 PM
4:00 PM
5:00 PM
6:00 PM
7:00 PM
8:00 PM
9:00 PM
10:00 PM
11:00 PM
12:00 AM

Daily Affirmation / Prayer / Inspirational Quote	Hours Slept

Excercise	Time Spent	Water	Daily Goals
		○ ○ ○ ○	
		○ ○ ○ ○	
		○ ○ ○ ○	

Nutritional Journal

	Nourishing Meals	Supplements/Essential Oils
BRKFST		
LNCH		
DNR		

Greens ○ Beans ○ Onions ○ Mushroom ○ Berries ○ Seeds ○

My Daily Planner

My Schedule for __/__/__

6:00 AM
7:00 AM
8:00 AM
9:00 AM
10:00 AM
11:00 AM
12:00 PM
1:00 PM
2:00 PM
3:00 PM
4:00 PM
5:00 PM
6:00 PM
7:00 PM
8:00 PM
9:00 PM
10:00 PM
11:00 PM
12:00 AM

Daily Affirmation / Prayer / Inspirational Quote	Hours Slept

Excercise	Time Spent	Water	Daily Goals
		○ ○ ○ ○	
		○ ○ ○ ○	
		○ ○ ○ ○	

Nutritional Journal

	Nourishing Meals	Supplements/Essential Oils
BRKFST		
LNCH		
DNR		

Greens ○ Beans ○ Onions ○ Mushroom ○ Berries ○ Seeds ○

My Daily Planner

My Schedule for __/__/__

6:00 AM	
7:00 AM	
8:00 AM	
9:00 AM	
10:00 AM	
11:00 AM	
12:00 PM	
1:00 PM	
2:00 PM	
3:00 PM	
4:00 PM	
5:00 PM	
6:00 PM	
7:00 PM	
8:00 PM	
9:00 PM	
10:00 PM	
11:00 PM	
12:00 AM	

Daily Affirmation / Prayer / Inspirational Quote	Hours Slept

Excercise	Time Spent

Water ○ ○ ○ ○ ○ ○ ○ ○ ○ ○ ○ ○

Daily Goals

Nutritional Journal

	Nourishing Meals	Supplements/Essential Oils
BRKFST		
LNCH		
DNR		

Greens ○ Beans ○ Onions ○ Mushroom ○ Berries ○ Seeds ○

My Daily Planner

My Schedule for __/__/__

6:00 AM	
7:00 AM	
8:00 AM	
9:00 AM	
10:00 AM	
11:00 AM	
12:00 PM	
1:00 PM	
2:00 PM	
3:00 PM	
4:00 PM	
5:00 PM	
6:00 PM	
7:00 PM	
8:00 PM	
9:00 PM	
10:00 PM	
11:00 PM	
12:00 AM	

Daily Affirmation / Prayer / Inspirational Quote	Hours Slept

Excercise	Time Spent	Water	Daily Goals
		○ ○ ○ ○	
		○ ○ ○ ○	
		○ ○ ○ ○	

Nutritional Journal

	Nourishing Meals	Supplements/Essential Oils
BRKFST		
LNCH		
DNR		

Greens ○ Beans ○ Onions ○ Mushroom ○ Berries ○ Seeds ○

My Daily Planner

My Schedule for __/__/__

6:00 AM
7:00 AM
8:00 AM
9:00 AM
10:00 AM
11:00 AM
12:00 PM
1:00 PM
2:00 PM
3:00 PM
4:00 PM
5:00 PM
6:00 PM
7:00 PM
8:00 PM
9:00 PM
10:00 PM
11:00 PM
12:00 AM

Daily Affirmation / Prayer / Inspirational Quote	Hours Slept

Excercise	Time Spent	Water	Daily Goals
		○ ○ ○ ○	
		○ ○ ○ ○	
		○ ○ ○ ○	

Nutritional Journal

	Nourishing Meals	Supplements/Essential Oils
BRKFST		
LNCH		
DNR		

Greens ○ Beans ○ Onions ○ Mushroom ○ Berries ○ Seeds ○

My Weekly Planner

My Categories	Monday __/__/__	Tuesday __/__/__	Wednesday __/__/__

My Weekly Planner

Thursday __/__/__	Friday __/__/__	Saturday __/__/__	Sunday __/__/__

My Meal Planner

For Week of / /

	Breakfast	Lunch	Dinner	Groceries
Monday				
Tuesday				
Wednesday				
Thursday				
Friday				
Saturday				
Sunday				

Special Instructions and Notes

My Daily Planner

My Schedule for __/__/__

6:00 AM	
7:00 AM	
8:00 AM	
9:00 AM	
10:00 AM	
11:00 AM	
12:00 PM	
1:00 PM	
2:00 PM	
3:00 PM	
4:00 PM	
5:00 PM	
6:00 PM	
7:00 PM	
8:00 PM	
9:00 PM	
10:00 PM	
11:00 PM	
12:00 AM	

Daily Affirmation / Prayer / Inspirational Quote	Hours Slept

Excercise	Time Spent	Water	Daily Goals
		○ ○ ○ ○	
		○ ○ ○ ○	
		○ ○ ○ ○	

Nutritional Journal		
	Nourishing Meals	Supplements/Essential Oils
BRKFST		
LNCH		
DNR		

Greens ○ Beans ○ Onions ○ Mushroom ○ Berries ○ Seeds ○

My Daily Planner

My Schedule for __/__/__

6:00 AM	
7:00 AM	
8:00 AM	
9:00 AM	
10:00 AM	
11:00 AM	
12:00 PM	
1:00 PM	
2:00 PM	
3:00 PM	
4:00 PM	
5:00 PM	
6:00 PM	
7:00 PM	
8:00 PM	
9:00 PM	
10:00 PM	
11:00 PM	
12:00 AM	

Daily Affirmation / Prayer / Inspirational Quote	Hours Slept

Excercise	Time Spent	Water	Daily Goals
		○ ○ ○ ○	
		○ ○ ○ ○	
		○ ○ ○ ○	

Nutritional Journal

	Nourishing Meals	Supplements/Essential Oils
BRKFST		
LNCH		
DNR		

Greens ○ Beans ○ Onions ○ Mushroom ○ Berries ○ Seeds ○

My Daily Planner

My Schedule for __/__/__

6:00 AM	
7:00 AM	
8:00 AM	
9:00 AM	
10:00 AM	
11:00 AM	
12:00 PM	
1:00 PM	
2:00 PM	
3:00 PM	
4:00 PM	
5:00 PM	
6:00 PM	
7:00 PM	
8:00 PM	
9:00 PM	
10:00 PM	
11:00 PM	
12:00 AM	

Daily Affirmation / Prayer / Inspirational Quote	Hours Slept

Excercise	Time Spent	Water	Daily Goals
		O O O O	
		O O O O	
		O O O O	

Nutritional Journal		
	Nourishing Meals	Supplements/Essential Oils
BRKFST		
LNCH		
DNR		

Greens O Beans O Onions O Mushroom O Berries O Seeds O

My Daily Planner

My Schedule for __/__/__

6:00 AM	
7:00 AM	
8:00 AM	
9:00 AM	
10:00 AM	
11:00 AM	
12:00 PM	
1:00 PM	
2:00 PM	
3:00 PM	
4:00 PM	
5:00 PM	
6:00 PM	
7:00 PM	
8:00 PM	
9:00 PM	
10:00 PM	
11:00 PM	
12:00 AM	

Daily Affirmation / Prayer / Inspirational Quote	Hours Slept

Excercise	Time Spent

Water

○ ○ ○ ○
○ ○ ○ ○
○ ○ ○ ○

Daily Goals

Nutritional Journal

	Nourishing Meals	Supplements/Essential Oils
BRKFST		
LNCH		
DNR		

Greens ○ Beans ○ Onions ○ Mushroom ○ Berries ○ Seeds ○

My Daily Planner

My Schedule for __/__/__

6:00 AM	
7:00 AM	
8:00 AM	
9:00 AM	
10:00 AM	
11:00 AM	
12:00 PM	
1:00 PM	
2:00 PM	
3:00 PM	
4:00 PM	
5:00 PM	
6:00 PM	
7:00 PM	
8:00 PM	
9:00 PM	
10:00 PM	
11:00 PM	
12:00 AM	

Daily Affirmation / Prayer / Inspirational Quote	Hours Slept

Excercise	Time Spent	Water	Daily Goals
		O O O O	
		O O O O	
		O O O O	

Nutritional Journal

	Nourishing Meals	Supplements/Essential Oils
BRKFST		
LNCH		
DNR		

Greens O Beans O Onions O Mushroom O Berries O Seeds O

My Daily Planner

My Schedule for __/__/__

6:00 AM
7:00 AM
8:00 AM
9:00 AM
10:00 AM
11:00 AM
12:00 PM
1:00 PM
2:00 PM
3:00 PM
4:00 PM
5:00 PM
6:00 PM
7:00 PM
8:00 PM
9:00 PM
10:00 PM
11:00 PM
12:00 AM

Daily Affirmation / Prayer / Inspirational Quote	Hours Slept

Excercise	Time Spent	Water	Daily Goals
		○ ○ ○ ○	
		○ ○ ○ ○	
		○ ○ ○ ○	

Nutritional Journal

	Nourishing Meals	Supplements/Essential Oils
BRKFST		
LNCH		
DNR		

Greens ○ Beans ○ Onions ○ Mushroom ○ Berries ○ Seeds ○

My Daily Planner

My Schedule for __/__/__

6:00 AM	
7:00 AM	
8:00 AM	
9:00 AM	
10:00 AM	
11:00 AM	
12:00 PM	
1:00 PM	
2:00 PM	
3:00 PM	
4:00 PM	
5:00 PM	
6:00 PM	
7:00 PM	
8:00 PM	
9:00 PM	
10:00 PM	
11:00 PM	
12:00 AM	

Daily Affirmation / Prayer / Inspirational Quote	Hours Slept

Excercise	Time Spent	Water	Daily Goals
		○ ○ ○ ○	
		○ ○ ○ ○	
		○ ○ ○ ○	

Nutritional Journal

	Nourishing Meals	Supplements/Essential Oils
BRKFST		
LNCH		
DNR		

Greens ○ Beans ○ Onions ○ Mushroom ○ Berries ○ Seeds ○

My Weekly Planner

My Categories	Monday _/_/_	Tuesday _/_/_	Wednesday _/_/_

My Weekly Planner

Thursday __/__/__	Friday __/__/__	Saturday __/__/__	Sunday __/__/__

My Meal Planner

For Week of / /

	Breakfast	Lunch	Dinner	Groceries
Monday				
Tuesday				
Wednesday				
Thursday				
Friday				
Saturday				
Sunday				

Special Instructions and Notes

My Daily Planner

My Schedule for __/__/__

6:00 AM	
7:00 AM	
8:00 AM	
9:00 AM	
10:00 AM	
11:00 AM	
12:00 PM	
1:00 PM	
2:00 PM	
3:00 PM	
4:00 PM	
5:00 PM	
6:00 PM	
7:00 PM	
8:00 PM	
9:00 PM	
10:00 PM	
11:00 PM	
12:00 AM	

Daily Affirmation / Prayer / Inspirational Quote	Hours Slept

Excercise	Time Spent	Water	Daily Goals
		○ ○ ○ ○	
		○ ○ ○ ○	
		○ ○ ○ ○	

Nutritional Journal

	Nourishing Meals	Supplements/Essential Oils
BRKFST		
LNCH		
DNR		

Greens ○ Beans ○ Onions ○ Mushroom ○ Berries ○ Seeds ○

My Daily Planner

My Schedule for __/__/__

6:00 AM	
7:00 AM	
8:00 AM	
9:00 AM	
10:00 AM	
11:00 AM	
12:00 PM	
1:00 PM	
2:00 PM	
3:00 PM	
4:00 PM	
5:00 PM	
6:00 PM	
7:00 PM	
8:00 PM	
9:00 PM	
10:00 PM	
11:00 PM	
12:00 AM	

Daily Affirmation / Prayer / Inspirational Quote	Hours Slept

Excercise	Time Spent	Water	Daily Goals
		○ ○ ○ ○	
		○ ○ ○ ○	
		○ ○ ○ ○	

Nutritional Journal

	Nourishing Meals	Supplements/Essential Oils
BRKFST		
LNCH		
DNR		

Greens ○ Beans ○ Onions ○ Mushroom ○ Berries ○ Seeds ○

My Daily Planner

My Schedule for __/__/__

6:00 AM	
7:00 AM	
8:00 AM	
9:00 AM	
10:00 AM	
11:00 AM	
12:00 PM	
1:00 PM	
2:00 PM	
3:00 PM	
4:00 PM	
5:00 PM	
6:00 PM	
7:00 PM	
8:00 PM	
9:00 PM	
10:00 PM	
11:00 PM	
12:00 AM	

Daily Affirmation / Prayer / Inspirational Quote	Hours Slept

Excercise	Time Spent	Water	Daily Goals
		○ ○ ○ ○	
		○ ○ ○ ○	
		○ ○ ○ ○	

Nutritional Journal

	Nourishing Meals	Supplements/Essential Oils
BRKFST		
LNCH		
DNR		

Greens ○ Beans ○ Onions ○ Mushroom ○ Berries ○ Seeds ○

My Daily Planner

My Schedule for __/__/__

6:00 AM	
7:00 AM	
8:00 AM	
9:00 AM	
10:00 AM	
11:00 AM	
12:00 PM	
1:00 PM	
2:00 PM	
3:00 PM	
4:00 PM	
5:00 PM	
6:00 PM	
7:00 PM	
8:00 PM	
9:00 PM	
10:00 PM	
11:00 PM	
12:00 AM	

Daily Affirmation / Prayer / Inspirational Quote	Hours Slept

Excercise	Time Spent	Water	Daily Goals
		O O O O	
		O O O O	
		O O O O	

Nutritional Journal

	Nourishing Meals	Supplements/Essential Oils
BRKFST		
LNCH		
DNR		

Greens O Beans O Onions O Mushroom O Berries O Seeds O

My Daily Planner

My Schedule for __/__/__

6:00 AM	
7:00 AM	
8:00 AM	
9:00 AM	
10:00 AM	
11:00 AM	
12:00 PM	
1:00 PM	
2:00 PM	
3:00 PM	
4:00 PM	
5:00 PM	
6:00 PM	
7:00 PM	
8:00 PM	
9:00 PM	
10:00 PM	
11:00 PM	
12:00 AM	

Daily Affirmation / Prayer / Inspirational Quote	Hours Slept

Excercise	Time Spent

Water			
○	○	○	○
○	○	○	○
○	○	○	○

Daily Goals

Nutritional Journal

	Nourishing Meals	Supplements/Essential Oils
BRKFST		
LNCH		
DNR		

Greens ○ Beans ○ Onions ○ Mushroom ○ Berries ○ Seeds ○

My Daily Planner

My Schedule for __/__/__

6:00 AM
7:00 AM
8:00 AM
9:00 AM
10:00 AM
11:00 AM
12:00 PM
1:00 PM
2:00 PM
3:00 PM
4:00 PM
5:00 PM
6:00 PM
7:00 PM
8:00 PM
9:00 PM
10:00 PM
11:00 PM
12:00 AM

Daily Affirmation / Prayer / Inspirational Quote	Hours Slept

Excercise	Time Spent	Water	Daily Goals
		○ ○ ○ ○	
		○ ○ ○ ○	
		○ ○ ○ ○	

Nutritional Journal

	Nourishing Meals	Supplements/Essential Oils
BRKFST		
LNCH		
DNR		

Greens ○ Beans ○ Onions ○ Mushroom ○ Berries ○ Seeds ○

My Daily Planner

My Schedule for __/__/__

6:00 AM	
7:00 AM	
8:00 AM	
9:00 AM	
10:00 AM	
11:00 AM	
12:00 PM	
1:00 PM	
2:00 PM	
3:00 PM	
4:00 PM	
5:00 PM	
6:00 PM	
7:00 PM	
8:00 PM	
9:00 PM	
10:00 PM	
11:00 PM	
12:00 AM	

Daily Affirmation / Prayer / Inspirational Quote	Hours Slept

Excercise	Time Spent	Water	Daily Goals
		○ ○ ○ ○	
		○ ○ ○ ○	
		○ ○ ○ ○	

Nutritional Journal

	Nourishing Meals	Supplements/Essential Oils
BRKFST		
LNCH		
DNR		

Greens ○ Beans ○ Onions ○ Mushroom ○ Berries ○ Seeds ○

My Weekly Planner

My Categories	Monday __/__/__	Tuesday __/__/__	Wednesday __/__/__

My Weekly Planner

Thursday __/__/__	Friday __/__/__	Saturday __/__/__	Sunday __/__/__

My Meal Planner

For Week of / /

	Breakfast	Lunch	Dinner	Groceries
Monday				
Tuesday				
Wednesday				
Thursday				
Friday				
Saturday				
Sunday				

Special Instructions and Notes

My Daily Planner

My Schedule for __/__/__

6:00 AM	
7:00 AM	
8:00 AM	
9:00 AM	
10:00 AM	
11:00 AM	
12:00 PM	
1:00 PM	
2:00 PM	
3:00 PM	
4:00 PM	
5:00 PM	
6:00 PM	
7:00 PM	
8:00 PM	
9:00 PM	
10:00 PM	
11:00 PM	
12:00 AM	

Daily Affirmation / Prayer / Inspirational Quote	Hours Slept

Excercise	Time Spent	Water	Daily Goals
		○ ○ ○ ○	
		○ ○ ○ ○	
		○ ○ ○ ○	

Nutritional Journal		
	Nourishing Meals	Supplements/Essential Oils
BRKFST		
LNCH		
DNR		

Greens ○ Beans ○ Onions ○ Mushroom ○ Berries ○ Seeds ○

My Daily Planner

My Schedule for __/__/__

6:00 AM	
7:00 AM	
8:00 AM	
9:00 AM	
10:00 AM	
11:00 AM	
12:00 PM	
1:00 PM	
2:00 PM	
3:00 PM	
4:00 PM	
5:00 PM	
6:00 PM	
7:00 PM	
8:00 PM	
9:00 PM	
10:00 PM	
11:00 PM	
12:00 AM	

Daily Affirmation / Prayer / Inspirational Quote	Hours Slept

Excercise	Time Spent	Water	Daily Goals
		O O O O	
		O O O O	
		O O O O	

Nutritional Journal

	Nourishing Meals	Supplements/Essential Oils
BRKFST		
LNCH		
DNR		

Greens O Beans O Onions O Mushroom O Berries O Seeds O

My Daily Planner

My Schedule for __/__/__

6:00 AM
7:00 AM
8:00 AM
9:00 AM
10:00 AM
11:00 AM
12:00 PM
1:00 PM
2:00 PM
3:00 PM
4:00 PM
5:00 PM
6:00 PM
7:00 PM
8:00 PM
9:00 PM
10:00 PM
11:00 PM
12:00 AM

Daily Affirmation / Prayer / Inspirational Quote	Hours Slept

Excercise	Time Spent	Water	Daily Goals
		○ ○ ○ ○	
		○ ○ ○ ○	
		○ ○ ○ ○	

Nutritional Journal

	Nourishing Meals	Supplements/Essential Oils
BRKFST		
LNCH		
DNR		

Greens ○ Beans ○ Onions ○ Mushroom ○ Berries ○ Seeds ○

My Daily Planner

My Schedule for __/__/__

6:00 AM	
7:00 AM	
8:00 AM	
9:00 AM	
10:00 AM	
11:00 AM	
12:00 PM	
1:00 PM	
2:00 PM	
3:00 PM	
4:00 PM	
5:00 PM	
6:00 PM	
7:00 PM	
8:00 PM	
9:00 PM	
10:00 PM	
11:00 PM	
12:00 AM	

Daily Affirmation / Prayer / Inspirational Quote	Hours Slept

Excercise	Time Spent	Water	Daily Goals
		O O O O	
		O O O O	
		O O O O	

Nutritional Journal		
	Nourishing Meals	Supplements/Essential Oils
BRKFST		
LNCH		
DNR		

Greens O Beans O Onions O Mushroom O Berries O Seeds O

My Daily Planner

My Schedule for __/__/__

6:00 AM	
7:00 AM	
8:00 AM	
9:00 AM	
10:00 AM	
11:00 AM	
12:00 PM	
1:00 PM	
2:00 PM	
3:00 PM	
4:00 PM	
5:00 PM	
6:00 PM	
7:00 PM	
8:00 PM	
9:00 PM	
10:00 PM	
11:00 PM	
12:00 AM	

Daily Affirmation / Prayer / Inspirational Quote	Hours Slept

Excercise	Time Spent	Water	Daily Goals
		○ ○ ○ ○	
		○ ○ ○ ○	
		○ ○ ○ ○	

Nutritional Journal

	Nourishing Meals	Supplements/Essential Oils
BRKFST		
LNCH		
DNR		

Greens ○ Beans ○ Onions ○ Mushroom ○ Berries ○ Seeds ○

My Daily Planner

My Schedule for __/__/__

6:00 AM	
7:00 AM	
8:00 AM	
9:00 AM	
10:00 AM	
11:00 AM	
12:00 PM	
1:00 PM	
2:00 PM	
3:00 PM	
4:00 PM	
5:00 PM	
6:00 PM	
7:00 PM	
8:00 PM	
9:00 PM	
10:00 PM	
11:00 PM	
12:00 AM	

Daily Affirmation / Prayer / Inspirational Quote	Hours Slept

Excercise	Time Spent	Water	Daily Goals
		○ ○ ○ ○	
		○ ○ ○ ○	
		○ ○ ○ ○	

Nutritional Journal

	Nourishing Meals	Supplements/Essential Oils
BRKFST		
LNCH		
DNR		

Greens ○ Beans ○ Onions ○ Mushroom ○ Berries ○ Seeds ○

My Daily Planner

My Schedule for __/__/__

6:00 AM	
7:00 AM	
8:00 AM	
9:00 AM	
10:00 AM	
11:00 AM	
12:00 PM	
1:00 PM	
2:00 PM	
3:00 PM	
4:00 PM	
5:00 PM	
6:00 PM	
7:00 PM	
8:00 PM	
9:00 PM	
10:00 PM	
11:00 PM	
12:00 AM	

Daily Affirmation / Prayer / Inspirational Quote	Hours Slept

Excercise	Time Spent	Water	Daily Goals
		○ ○ ○ ○	
		○ ○ ○ ○	
		○ ○ ○ ○	

Nutritional Journal

	Nourishing Meals	Supplements/Essential Oils
BRKFST		
LNCH		
DNR		

Greens ○ Beans ○ Onions ○ Mushroom ○ Berries ○ Seeds ○

My Weekly Planner

My Categories	Monday __/__/__	Tuesday __/__/__	Wednesday __/__/__

My Weekly Planner

Thursday __/__/__	Friday __/__/__	Saturday __/__/__	Sunday __/__/__

My Meal Planner

For Week of / /

	Breakfast	Lunch	Dinner	Groceries
Monday				
Tuesday				
Wednesday				
Thursday				
Friday				
Saturday				
Sunday				

Special Instructions and Notes

My Daily Planner

My Schedule for __/__/__

6:00 AM	
7:00 AM	
8:00 AM	
9:00 AM	
10:00 AM	
11:00 AM	
12:00 PM	
1:00 PM	
2:00 PM	
3:00 PM	
4:00 PM	
5:00 PM	
6:00 PM	
7:00 PM	
8:00 PM	
9:00 PM	
10:00 PM	
11:00 PM	
12:00 AM	

Daily Affirmation / Prayer / Inspirational Quote	Hours Slept

Excercise	Time Spent	Water	Daily Goals
		○ ○ ○ ○	
		○ ○ ○ ○	
		○ ○ ○ ○	

Nutritional Journal

	Nourishing Meals	Supplements/Essential Oils
BRKFST		
LNCH		
DNR		

Greens ○ Beans ○ Onions ○ Mushroom ○ Berries ○ Seeds ○

My Daily Planner

My Schedule for __/__/__

6:00 AM	
7:00 AM	
8:00 AM	
9:00 AM	
10:00 AM	
11:00 AM	
12:00 PM	
1:00 PM	
2:00 PM	
3:00 PM	
4:00 PM	
5:00 PM	
6:00 PM	
7:00 PM	
8:00 PM	
9:00 PM	
10:00 PM	
11:00 PM	
12:00 AM	

Daily Affirmation / Prayer / Inspirational Quote	Hours Slept

Excercise	Time Spent	Water	Daily Goals
		○ ○ ○ ○	
		○ ○ ○ ○	
		○ ○ ○ ○	

Nutritional Journal		
	Nourishing Meals	Supplements/Essential Oils
BRKFST		
LNCH		
DNR		

Greens ○ Beans ○ Onions ○ Mushroom ○ Berries ○ Seeds ○

My Daily Planner

My Schedule for __/__/__

6:00 AM	
7:00 AM	
8:00 AM	
9:00 AM	
10:00 AM	
11:00 AM	
12:00 PM	
1:00 PM	
2:00 PM	
3:00 PM	
4:00 PM	
5:00 PM	
6:00 PM	
7:00 PM	
8:00 PM	
9:00 PM	
10:00 PM	
11:00 PM	
12:00 AM	

Daily Affirmation / Prayer / Inspirational Quote	Hours Slept

Excercise	Time Spent	Water				Daily Goals
		O	O	O	O	
		O	O	O	O	
		O	O	O	O	

Nutritional Journal		
	Nourishing Meals	Supplements/Essential Oils
BRKFST		
LNCH		
DNR		

Greens O Beans O Onions O Mushroom O Berries O Seeds O

My Daily Planner

My Schedule for __/__/__

6:00 AM	
7:00 AM	
8:00 AM	
9:00 AM	
10:00 AM	
11:00 AM	
12:00 PM	
1:00 PM	
2:00 PM	
3:00 PM	
4:00 PM	
5:00 PM	
6:00 PM	
7:00 PM	
8:00 PM	
9:00 PM	
10:00 PM	
11:00 PM	
12:00 AM	

Daily Affirmation / Prayer / Inspirational Quote	Hours Slept

Excercise	Time Spent	Water				Daily Goals
		O	O	O	O	
		O	O	O	O	
		O	O	O	O	

Nutritional Journal

	Nourishing Meals	Supplements/Essential Oils
BRKFST		
LNCH		
DNR		

Greens O Beans O Onions O Mushroom O Berries O Seeds O

My Daily Planner

My Schedule for __/__/__

6:00 AM	
7:00 AM	
8:00 AM	
9:00 AM	
10:00 AM	
11:00 AM	
12:00 PM	
1:00 PM	
2:00 PM	
3:00 PM	
4:00 PM	
5:00 PM	
6:00 PM	
7:00 PM	
8:00 PM	
9:00 PM	
10:00 PM	
11:00 PM	
12:00 AM	

Daily Affirmation / Prayer / Inspirational Quote	Hours Slept

Excercise	Time Spent	Water	Daily Goals
		○ ○ ○ ○	
		○ ○ ○ ○	
		○ ○ ○ ○	

Nutritional Journal

	Nourishing Meals	Supplements/Essential Oils
BRKFST		
LNCH		
DNR		

Greens ○ Beans ○ Onions ○ Mushroom ○ Berries ○ Seeds ○

My Daily Planner

My Schedule for __/__/__

6:00 AM	
7:00 AM	
8:00 AM	
9:00 AM	
10:00 AM	
11:00 AM	
12:00 PM	
1:00 PM	
2:00 PM	
3:00 PM	
4:00 PM	
5:00 PM	
6:00 PM	
7:00 PM	
8:00 PM	
9:00 PM	
10:00 PM	
11:00 PM	
12:00 AM	

Daily Affirmation / Prayer / Inspirational Quote	Hours Slept

Excercise	Time Spent	Water	Daily Goals
		○ ○ ○ ○	
		○ ○ ○ ○	
		○ ○ ○ ○	

Nutritional Journal

	Nourishing Meals	Supplements/Essential Oils
BRKFST		
LNCH		
DNR		

Greens ○ Beans ○ Onions ○ Mushroom ○ Berries ○ Seeds ○

My Daily Planner

My Schedule for __/__/__

6:00 AM
7:00 AM
8:00 AM
9:00 AM
10:00 AM
11:00 AM
12:00 PM
1:00 PM
2:00 PM
3:00 PM
4:00 PM
5:00 PM
6:00 PM
7:00 PM
8:00 PM
9:00 PM
10:00 PM
11:00 PM
12:00 AM

Daily Affirmation / Prayer / Inspirational Quote	Hours Slept

Excercise	Time Spent	Water	Daily Goals
		○ ○ ○ ○	
		○ ○ ○ ○	
		○ ○ ○ ○	

Nutritional Journal

	Nourishing Meals	Supplements/Essential Oils
BRKFST		
LNCH		
DNR		

Greens ○ Beans ○ Onions ○ Mushroom ○ Berries ○ Seeds ○

My Monthly Planner

MONTH ____________________

Monday	Tuesday	Wednesday	Thursday

Healthy You Measurements			
Chest		Upper Arm	
Waist		Thigh	
Hips		Calf	

My Monthly Planner

MONTH ______________________

Friday	Saturday	Sunday	Special Notes

My Fitness Goals

My Weekly Planner

My Categories	Monday __/__/__	Tuesday __/__/__	Wednesday __/__/__

My Weekly Planner

Thursday __/__/__	Friday __/__/__	Saturday __/__/__	Sunday __/__/__

My Meal Planner

	For Week of / /			
	Breakfast	Lunch	Dinner	Groceries
Monday				
Tuesday				
Wednesday				
Thursday				
Friday				
Saturday				
Sunday				

Special Instructions and Notes

My Daily Planner

My Schedule for __/__/__

6:00 AM	
7:00 AM	
8:00 AM	
9:00 AM	
10:00 AM	
11:00 AM	
12:00 PM	
1:00 PM	
2:00 PM	
3:00 PM	
4:00 PM	
5:00 PM	
6:00 PM	
7:00 PM	
8:00 PM	
9:00 PM	
10:00 PM	
11:00 PM	
12:00 AM	

Daily Affirmation / Prayer / Inspirational Quote	Hours Slept

Excercise	Time Spent	Water				Daily Goals
		O	O	O	O	
		O	O	O	O	
		O	O	O	O	

Nutritional Journal

	Nourishing Meals	Supplements/Essential Oils
BRKFST		
LNCH		
DNR		

Greens O Beans O Onions O Mushroom O Berries O Seeds O

My Daily Planner

My Schedule for __/__/__

6:00 AM	
7:00 AM	
8:00 AM	
9:00 AM	
10:00 AM	
11:00 AM	
12:00 PM	
1:00 PM	
2:00 PM	
3:00 PM	
4:00 PM	
5:00 PM	
6:00 PM	
7:00 PM	
8:00 PM	
9:00 PM	
10:00 PM	
11:00 PM	
12:00 AM	

Daily Affirmation / Prayer / Inspirational Quote	Hours Slept

Excercise	Time Spent	Water	Daily Goals
		○ ○ ○ ○	
		○ ○ ○ ○	
		○ ○ ○ ○	

Nutritional Journal

	Nourishing Meals	Supplements/Essential Oils
BRKFST		
LNCH		
DNR		

Greens ○ Beans ○ Onions ○ Mushroom ○ Berries ○ Seeds ○

My Daily Planner

My Schedule for __/__/__

6:00 AM
7:00 AM
8:00 AM
9:00 AM
10:00 AM
11:00 AM
12:00 PM
1:00 PM
2:00 PM
3:00 PM
4:00 PM
5:00 PM
6:00 PM
7:00 PM
8:00 PM
9:00 PM
10:00 PM
11:00 PM
12:00 AM

Daily Affirmation / Prayer / Inspirational Quote	Hours Slept

Excercise	Time Spent	Water	Daily Goals
		○ ○ ○ ○	
		○ ○ ○ ○	
		○ ○ ○ ○	

Nutritional Journal

	Nourishing Meals	Supplements/Essential Oils
BRKFST		
LNCH		
DNR		

Greens ○ Beans ○ Onions ○ Mushroom ○ Berries ○ Seeds ○

My Daily Planner

My Schedule for __/__/__

6:00 AM
7:00 AM
8:00 AM
9:00 AM
10:00 AM
11:00 AM
12:00 PM
1:00 PM
2:00 PM
3:00 PM
4:00 PM
5:00 PM
6:00 PM
7:00 PM
8:00 PM
9:00 PM
10:00 PM
11:00 PM
12:00 AM

Daily Affirmation / Prayer / Inspirational Quote	Hours Slept

Excercise	Time Spent	Water	Daily Goals
		○ ○ ○ ○	
		○ ○ ○ ○	
		○ ○ ○ ○	

Nutritional Journal		
	Nourishing Meals	Supplements/Essential Oils
BRKFST		
LNCH		
DNR		

Greens ○ Beans ○ Onions ○ Mushroom ○ Berries ○ Seeds ○

My Daily Planner

My Schedule for __/__/__

6:00 AM	
7:00 AM	
8:00 AM	
9:00 AM	
10:00 AM	
11:00 AM	
12:00 PM	
1:00 PM	
2:00 PM	
3:00 PM	
4:00 PM	
5:00 PM	
6:00 PM	
7:00 PM	
8:00 PM	
9:00 PM	
10:00 PM	
11:00 PM	
12:00 AM	

Daily Affirmation / Prayer / Inspirational Quote	Hours Slept

Excercise	Time Spent	Water	Daily Goals
		○ ○ ○ ○	
		○ ○ ○ ○	
		○ ○ ○ ○	

Nutritional Journal		
	Nourishing Meals	Supplements/Essential Oils
BRKFST		
LNCH		
DNR		

Greens ○ Beans ○ Onions ○ Mushroom ○ Berries ○ Seeds ○

My Daily Planner

My Schedule for __/__/__

6:00 AM	
7:00 AM	
8:00 AM	
9:00 AM	
10:00 AM	
11:00 AM	
12:00 PM	
1:00 PM	
2:00 PM	
3:00 PM	
4:00 PM	
5:00 PM	
6:00 PM	
7:00 PM	
8:00 PM	
9:00 PM	
10:00 PM	
11:00 PM	
12:00 AM	

Daily Affirmation / Prayer / Inspirational Quote	Hours Slept

Excercise	Time Spent	Water				Daily Goals
		O	O	O	O	
		O	O	O	O	
		O	O	O	O	

Nutritional Journal		
	Nourishing Meals	Supplements/Essential Oils
BRKFST		
LNCH		
DNR		

Greens O Beans O Onions O Mushroom O Berries O Seeds O

My Daily Planner

My Schedule for __/__/__

6:00 AM	
7:00 AM	
8:00 AM	
9:00 AM	
10:00 AM	
11:00 AM	
12:00 PM	
1:00 PM	
2:00 PM	
3:00 PM	
4:00 PM	
5:00 PM	
6:00 PM	
7:00 PM	
8:00 PM	
9:00 PM	
10:00 PM	
11:00 PM	
12:00 AM	

Daily Affirmation / Prayer / Inspirational Quote	Hours Slept

Excercise	Time Spent	Water	Daily Goals
		○ ○ ○ ○	
		○ ○ ○ ○	
		○ ○ ○ ○	

Nutritional Journal

	Nourishing Meals	Supplements/Essential Oils
BRKFST		
LNCH		
DNR		

Greens ○ Beans ○ Onions ○ Mushroom ○ Berries ○ Seeds ○

My Weekly Planner

My Categories	Monday __/__/__	Tuesday __/__/__	Wednesday __/__/__

My Weekly Planner

Thursday __/__/__	Friday __/__/__	Saturday __/__/__	Sunday __/__/__

My Meal Planner

For Week of / /

	Breakfast	Lunch	Dinner	Groceries
Monday				
Tuesday				
Wednesday				
Thursday				
Friday				
Saturday				
Sunday				

Special Instructions and Notes

My Daily Planner

My Schedule for __/__/__

6:00 AM	
7:00 AM	
8:00 AM	
9:00 AM	
10:00 AM	
11:00 AM	
12:00 PM	
1:00 PM	
2:00 PM	
3:00 PM	
4:00 PM	
5:00 PM	
6:00 PM	
7:00 PM	
8:00 PM	
9:00 PM	
10:00 PM	
11:00 PM	
12:00 AM	

Daily Affirmation / Prayer / Inspirational Quote	Hours Slept

Excercise	Time Spent	Water				Daily Goals
		O	O	O	O	
		O	O	O	O	
		O	O	O	O	

Nutritional Journal		
	Nourishing Meals	Supplements/Essential Oils
BRKFST		
LNCH		
DNR		

Greens O Beans O Onions O Mushroom O Berries O Seeds O

My Daily Planner

My Schedule for __/__/__

6:00 AM	
7:00 AM	
8:00 AM	
9:00 AM	
10:00 AM	
11:00 AM	
12:00 PM	
1:00 PM	
2:00 PM	
3:00 PM	
4:00 PM	
5:00 PM	
6:00 PM	
7:00 PM	
8:00 PM	
9:00 PM	
10:00 PM	
11:00 PM	
12:00 AM	

Daily Affirmation / Prayer / Inspirational Quote	Hours Slept

Excercise	Time Spent	Water	Daily Goals
		O O O O	
		O O O O	
		O O O O	

Nutritional Journal

	Nourishing Meals	Supplements/Essential Oils
BRKFST		
LNCH		
DNR		

Greens O Beans O Onions O Mushroom O Berries O Seeds O

My Daily Planner

My Schedule for __/__/__

6:00 AM	
7:00 AM	
8:00 AM	
9:00 AM	
10:00 AM	
11:00 AM	
12:00 PM	
1:00 PM	
2:00 PM	
3:00 PM	
4:00 PM	
5:00 PM	
6:00 PM	
7:00 PM	
8:00 PM	
9:00 PM	
10:00 PM	
11:00 PM	
12:00 AM	

Daily Affirmation / Prayer / Inspirational Quote	Hours Slept

Excercise	Time Spent	Water	Daily Goals
		○ ○ ○ ○	
		○ ○ ○ ○	
		○ ○ ○ ○	

Nutritional Journal

	Nourishing Meals	Supplements/Essential Oils
BRKFST		
LNCH		
DNR		

Greens ○ Beans ○ Onions ○ Mushroom ○ Berries ○ Seeds ○

My Daily Planner

My Schedule for __/__/__

6:00 AM	
7:00 AM	
8:00 AM	
9:00 AM	
10:00 AM	
11:00 AM	
12:00 PM	
1:00 PM	
2:00 PM	
3:00 PM	
4:00 PM	
5:00 PM	
6:00 PM	
7:00 PM	
8:00 PM	
9:00 PM	
10:00 PM	
11:00 PM	
12:00 AM	

Daily Affirmation / Prayer / Inspirational Quote	Hours Slept

Excercise	Time Spent	Water	Daily Goals
		○ ○ ○ ○	
		○ ○ ○ ○	
		○ ○ ○ ○	

Nutritional Journal

	Nourishing Meals	Supplements/Essential Oils
BRKFST		
LNCH		
DNR		

Greens ○ Beans ○ Onions ○ Mushroom ○ Berries ○ Seeds ○

My Daily Planner

My Schedule for __/__/__

6:00 AM
7:00 AM
8:00 AM
9:00 AM
10:00 AM
11:00 AM
12:00 PM
1:00 PM
2:00 PM
3:00 PM
4:00 PM
5:00 PM
6:00 PM
7:00 PM
8:00 PM
9:00 PM
10:00 PM
11:00 PM
12:00 AM

Daily Affirmation / Prayer / Inspirational Quote	Hours Slept

Excercise	Time Spent	Water	Daily Goals
		○ ○ ○ ○	
		○ ○ ○ ○	
		○ ○ ○ ○	

Nutritional Journal

	Nourishing Meals	Supplements/Essential Oils
BRKFST		
LNCH		
DNR		

Greens ○ Beans ○ Onions ○ Mushroom ○ Berries ○ Seeds ○

My Daily Planner

My Schedule for __/__/__

6:00 AM	
7:00 AM	
8:00 AM	
9:00 AM	
10:00 AM	
11:00 AM	
12:00 PM	
1:00 PM	
2:00 PM	
3:00 PM	
4:00 PM	
5:00 PM	
6:00 PM	
7:00 PM	
8:00 PM	
9:00 PM	
10:00 PM	
11:00 PM	
12:00 AM	

Daily Affirmation / Prayer / Inspirational Quote	Hours Slept

Excercise	Time Spent	Water	Daily Goals
		O O O O	
		O O O O	
		O O O O	

Nutritional Journal

	Nourishing Meals	Supplements/Essential Oils
BRKFST		
LNCH		
DNR		

Greens O Beans O Onions O Mushroom O Berries O Seeds O

My Daily Planner

My Schedule for __/__/__

6:00 AM	
7:00 AM	
8:00 AM	
9:00 AM	
10:00 AM	
11:00 AM	
12:00 PM	
1:00 PM	
2:00 PM	
3:00 PM	
4:00 PM	
5:00 PM	
6:00 PM	
7:00 PM	
8:00 PM	
9:00 PM	
10:00 PM	
11:00 PM	
12:00 AM	

Daily Affirmation / Prayer / Inspirational Quote	Hours Slept

Excercise	Time Spent	Water	Daily Goals
		○ ○ ○ ○	
		○ ○ ○ ○	
		○ ○ ○ ○	

Nutritional Journal		
	Nourishing Meals	Supplements/Essential Oils
BRKFST		
LNCH		
DNR		

Greens ○ Beans ○ Onions ○ Mushroom ○ Berries ○ Seeds ○

My Weekly Planner

My Categories	Monday __/__/__	Tuesday __/__/__	Wednesday __/__/__

My Weekly Planner

Thursday __/__/__	Friday __/__/__	Saturday __/__/__	Sunday __/__/__

My Meal Planner

For Week of / /

	Breakfast	Lunch	Dinner	Groceries
Monday				
Tuesday				
Wednesday				
Thursday				
Friday				
Saturday				
Sunday				

Special Instructions and Notes

My Daily Planner

My Schedule for __/__/__

6:00 AM	
7:00 AM	
8:00 AM	
9:00 AM	
10:00 AM	
11:00 AM	
12:00 PM	
1:00 PM	
2:00 PM	
3:00 PM	
4:00 PM	
5:00 PM	
6:00 PM	
7:00 PM	
8:00 PM	
9:00 PM	
10:00 PM	
11:00 PM	
12:00 AM	

Daily Affirmation / Prayer / Inspirational Quote	Hours Slept

Excercise	Time Spent	Water	Daily Goals
		○ ○ ○ ○	
		○ ○ ○ ○	
		○ ○ ○ ○	

Nutritional Journal

	Nourishing Meals	Supplements/Essential Oils
BRKFST		
LNCH		
DNR		

Greens ○ Beans ○ Onions ○ Mushroom ○ Berries ○ Seeds ○

My Daily Planner

My Schedule for __/__/__

6:00 AM	
7:00 AM	
8:00 AM	
9:00 AM	
10:00 AM	
11:00 AM	
12:00 PM	
1:00 PM	
2:00 PM	
3:00 PM	
4:00 PM	
5:00 PM	
6:00 PM	
7:00 PM	
8:00 PM	
9:00 PM	
10:00 PM	
11:00 PM	
12:00 AM	

Daily Affirmation / Prayer / Inspirational Quote	Hours Slept

Excercise	Time Spent	Water	Daily Goals
		○ ○ ○ ○	
		○ ○ ○ ○	
		○ ○ ○ ○	

Nutritional Journal

	Nourishing Meals	Supplements/Essential Oils
BRKFST		
LNCH		
DNR		

Greens ○ Beans ○ Onions ○ Mushroom ○ Berries ○ Seeds ○

My Daily Planner

My Schedule for __/__/__

6:00 AM	
7:00 AM	
8:00 AM	
9:00 AM	
10:00 AM	
11:00 AM	
12:00 PM	
1:00 PM	
2:00 PM	
3:00 PM	
4:00 PM	
5:00 PM	
6:00 PM	
7:00 PM	
8:00 PM	
9:00 PM	
10:00 PM	
11:00 PM	
12:00 AM	

Daily Affirmation / Prayer / Inspirational Quote	Hours Slept

Excercise	Time Spent	Water	Daily Goals
		○ ○ ○ ○	
		○ ○ ○ ○	
		○ ○ ○ ○	

Nutritional Journal

	Nourishing Meals	Supplements/Essential Oils
BRKFST		
LNCH		
DNR		

Greens ○ Beans ○ Onions ○ Mushroom ○ Berries ○ Seeds ○

My Daily Planner

My Schedule for __/__/__

6:00 AM	
7:00 AM	
8:00 AM	
9:00 AM	
10:00 AM	
11:00 AM	
12:00 PM	
1:00 PM	
2:00 PM	
3:00 PM	
4:00 PM	
5:00 PM	
6:00 PM	
7:00 PM	
8:00 PM	
9:00 PM	
10:00 PM	
11:00 PM	
12:00 AM	

Daily Affirmation / Prayer / Inspirational Quote	Hours Slept

Excercise	Time Spent	Water	Daily Goals
		O O O O	
		O O O O	
		O O O O	

Nutritional Journal

	Nourishing Meals	Supplements/Essential Oils
BRKFST		
LNCH		
DNR		

Greens O Beans O Onions O Mushroom O Berries O Seeds O

My Daily Planner

My Schedule for __/__/__

6:00 AM
7:00 AM
8:00 AM
9:00 AM
10:00 AM
11:00 AM
12:00 PM
1:00 PM
2:00 PM
3:00 PM
4:00 PM
5:00 PM
6:00 PM
7:00 PM
8:00 PM
9:00 PM
10:00 PM
11:00 PM
12:00 AM

Daily Affirmation / Prayer / Inspirational Quote	Hours Slept

Excercise	Time Spent	Water	Daily Goals
		○ ○ ○ ○	
		○ ○ ○ ○	
		○ ○ ○ ○	

Nutritional Journal		
	Nourishing Meals	Supplements/Essential Oils
BRKFST		
LNCH		
DNR		

Greens ○ Beans ○ Onions ○ Mushroom ○ Berries ○ Seeds ○

My Daily Planner

My Schedule for ___/___/___

6:00 AM	
7:00 AM	
8:00 AM	
9:00 AM	
10:00 AM	
11:00 AM	
12:00 PM	
1:00 PM	
2:00 PM	
3:00 PM	
4:00 PM	
5:00 PM	
6:00 PM	
7:00 PM	
8:00 PM	
9:00 PM	
10:00 PM	
11:00 PM	
12:00 AM	

Daily Affirmation / Prayer / Inspirational Quote	Hours Slept

Excercise	Time Spent	Water	Daily Goals
		○ ○ ○ ○	
		○ ○ ○ ○	
		○ ○ ○ ○	

Nutritional Journal

	Nourishing Meals	Supplements/Essential Oils
BRKFST		
LNCH		
DNR		

Greens ○ Beans ○ Onions ○ Mushroom ○ Berries ○ Seeds ○

My Daily Planner

My Schedule for __/__/__

6:00 AM	
7:00 AM	
8:00 AM	
9:00 AM	
10:00 AM	
11:00 AM	
12:00 PM	
1:00 PM	
2:00 PM	
3:00 PM	
4:00 PM	
5:00 PM	
6:00 PM	
7:00 PM	
8:00 PM	
9:00 PM	
10:00 PM	
11:00 PM	
12:00 AM	

Daily Affirmation / Prayer / Inspirational Quote	Hours Slept

Excercise	Time Spent	Water	Daily Goals
		○ ○ ○ ○	
		○ ○ ○ ○	
		○ ○ ○ ○	

Nutritional Journal

	Nourishing Meals	Supplements/Essential Oils
BRKFST		
LNCH		
DNR		

Greens ○ Beans ○ Onions ○ Mushroom ○ Berries ○ Seeds ○

My Weekly Planner

My Categories	Monday __/__/__	Tuesday __/__/__	Wednesday __/__/__

My Weekly Planner

Thursday __/__/__	Friday __/__/__	Saturday __/__/__	Sunday __/__/__

My Meal Planner

For Week of / /

	Breakfast	Lunch	Dinner	Groceries
Monday				
Tuesday				
Wednesday				
Thursday				
Friday				
Saturday				
Sunday				

Special Instructions and Notes

My Daily Planner

My Schedule for __/__/__

6:00 AM
7:00 AM
8:00 AM
9:00 AM
10:00 AM
11:00 AM
12:00 PM
1:00 PM
2:00 PM
3:00 PM
4:00 PM
5:00 PM
6:00 PM
7:00 PM
8:00 PM
9:00 PM
10:00 PM
11:00 PM
12:00 AM

Daily Affirmation / Prayer / Inspirational Quote	Hours Slept

Excercise	Time Spent	Water	Daily Goals
		○ ○ ○ ○	
		○ ○ ○ ○	
		○ ○ ○ ○	

Nutritional Journal

	Nourishing Meals	Supplements/Essential Oils
BRKFST		
LNCH		
DNR		

Greens ○ Beans ○ Onions ○ Mushroom ○ Berries ○ Seeds ○

My Daily Planner

My Schedule for __/__/__

6:00 AM	
7:00 AM	
8:00 AM	
9:00 AM	
10:00 AM	
11:00 AM	
12:00 PM	
1:00 PM	
2:00 PM	
3:00 PM	
4:00 PM	
5:00 PM	
6:00 PM	
7:00 PM	
8:00 PM	
9:00 PM	
10:00 PM	
11:00 PM	
12:00 AM	

Daily Affirmation / Prayer / Inspirational Quote	Hours Slept

Excercise	Time Spent	Water	Daily Goals
		○ ○ ○ ○	
		○ ○ ○ ○	
		○ ○ ○ ○	

Nutritional Journal

	Nourishing Meals	Supplements/Essential Oils
BRKFST		
LNCH		
DNR		

Greens ○ Beans ○ Onions ○ Mushroom ○ Berries ○ Seeds ○

My Daily Planner

My Schedule for __/__/__

6:00 AM	
7:00 AM	
8:00 AM	
9:00 AM	
10:00 AM	
11:00 AM	
12:00 PM	
1:00 PM	
2:00 PM	
3:00 PM	
4:00 PM	
5:00 PM	
6:00 PM	
7:00 PM	
8:00 PM	
9:00 PM	
10:00 PM	
11:00 PM	
12:00 AM	

Daily Affirmation / Prayer / Inspirational Quote	Hours Slept

Excercise	Time Spent	Water	Daily Goals
		○ ○ ○ ○	
		○ ○ ○ ○	
		○ ○ ○ ○	

Nutritional Journal

	Nourishing Meals	Supplements/Essential Oils
BRKFST		
LNCH		
DNR		

Greens ○ Beans ○ Onions ○ Mushroom ○ Berries ○ Seeds ○

My Daily Planner

My Schedule for __/__/__

6:00 AM	
7:00 AM	
8:00 AM	
9:00 AM	
10:00 AM	
11:00 AM	
12:00 PM	
1:00 PM	
2:00 PM	
3:00 PM	
4:00 PM	
5:00 PM	
6:00 PM	
7:00 PM	
8:00 PM	
9:00 PM	
10:00 PM	
11:00 PM	
12:00 AM	

Daily Affirmation / Prayer / Inspirational Quote	Hours Slept

Excercise	Time Spent	Water	Daily Goals
		○ ○ ○ ○	
		○ ○ ○ ○	
		○ ○ ○ ○	

Nutritional Journal

	Nourishing Meals	Supplements/Essential Oils
BRKFST		
LNCH		
DNR		

Greens ○ Beans ○ Onions ○ Mushroom ○ Berries ○ Seeds ○

My Daily Planner

My Schedule for __/__/__

6:00 AM	
7:00 AM	
8:00 AM	
9:00 AM	
10:00 AM	
11:00 AM	
12:00 PM	
1:00 PM	
2:00 PM	
3:00 PM	
4:00 PM	
5:00 PM	
6:00 PM	
7:00 PM	
8:00 PM	
9:00 PM	
10:00 PM	
11:00 PM	
12:00 AM	

Daily Affirmation / Prayer / Inspirational Quote	Hours Slept

Excercise	Time Spent	Water	Daily Goals
		○ ○ ○ ○	
		○ ○ ○ ○	
		○ ○ ○ ○	

Nutritional Journal

	Nourishing Meals	Supplements/Essential Oils
BRKFST		
LNCH		
DNR		

Greens ○ Beans ○ Onions ○ Mushroom ○ Berries ○ Seeds ○

My Daily Planner

My Schedule for __/__/__

6:00 AM
7:00 AM
8:00 AM
9:00 AM
10:00 AM
11:00 AM
12:00 PM
1:00 PM
2:00 PM
3:00 PM
4:00 PM
5:00 PM
6:00 PM
7:00 PM
8:00 PM
9:00 PM
10:00 PM
11:00 PM
12:00 AM

Daily Affirmation / Prayer / Inspirational Quote	Hours Slept

Excercise	Time Spent	Water	Daily Goals
		O O O O	
		O O O O	
		O O O O	

Nutritional Journal

	Nourishing Meals	Supplements/Essential Oils
BRKFST		
LNCH		
DNR		

Greens O Beans O Onions O Mushroom O Berries O Seeds O

My Daily Planner

My Schedule for __/__/__

6:00 AM	
7:00 AM	
8:00 AM	
9:00 AM	
10:00 AM	
11:00 AM	
12:00 PM	
1:00 PM	
2:00 PM	
3:00 PM	
4:00 PM	
5:00 PM	
6:00 PM	
7:00 PM	
8:00 PM	
9:00 PM	
10:00 PM	
11:00 PM	
12:00 AM	

Daily Affirmation / Prayer / Inspirational Quote	Hours Slept

Excercise	Time Spent	Water	Daily Goals
		○ ○ ○ ○	
		○ ○ ○ ○	
		○ ○ ○ ○	

Nutritional Journal

	Nourishing Meals	Supplements/Essential Oils
BRKFST		
LNCH		
DNR		

Greens ○ Beans ○ Onions ○ Mushroom ○ Berries ○ Seeds ○

My Weekly Planner

My Categories	Monday __/__/__	Tuesday __/__/__	Wednesday __/__/__

My Weekly Planner

Thursday __/__/__	Friday __/__/__	Saturday __/__/__	Sunday __/__/__

My Meal Planner

For Week of / /

	Breakfast	Lunch	Dinner	Groceries
Monday				
Tuesday				
Wednesday				
Thursday				
Friday				
Saturday				
Sunday				

Special Instructions and Notes

My Daily Planner

My Schedule for __/__/__

6:00 AM
7:00 AM
8:00 AM
9:00 AM
10:00 AM
11:00 AM
12:00 PM
1:00 PM
2:00 PM
3:00 PM
4:00 PM
5:00 PM
6:00 PM
7:00 PM
8:00 PM
9:00 PM
10:00 PM
11:00 PM
12:00 AM

Daily Affirmation / Prayer / Inspirational Quote	Hours Slept

Excercise	Time Spent	Water	Daily Goals
		○ ○ ○ ○	
		○ ○ ○ ○	
		○ ○ ○ ○	

Nutritional Journal

	Nourishing Meals	Supplements/Essential Oils
BRKFST		
LNCH		
DNR		

Greens ○ Beans ○ Onions ○ Mushroom ○ Berries ○ Seeds ○

My Daily Planner

My Schedule for __/__/__

6:00 AM	
7:00 AM	
8:00 AM	
9:00 AM	
10:00 AM	
11:00 AM	
12:00 PM	
1:00 PM	
2:00 PM	
3:00 PM	
4:00 PM	
5:00 PM	
6:00 PM	
7:00 PM	
8:00 PM	
9:00 PM	
10:00 PM	
11:00 PM	
12:00 AM	

Daily Affirmation / Prayer / Inspirational Quote	Hours Slept

Excercise	Time Spent	Water	Daily Goals
		○ ○ ○ ○	
		○ ○ ○ ○	
		○ ○ ○ ○	

Nutritional Journal

	Nourishing Meals	Supplements/Essential Oils
BRKFST		
LNCH		
DNR		

Greens ○ Beans ○ Onions ○ Mushroom ○ Berries ○ Seeds ○

My Daily Planner

My Schedule for __/__/__

6:00 AM
7:00 AM
8:00 AM
9:00 AM
10:00 AM
11:00 AM
12:00 PM
1:00 PM
2:00 PM
3:00 PM
4:00 PM
5:00 PM
6:00 PM
7:00 PM
8:00 PM
9:00 PM
10:00 PM
11:00 PM
12:00 AM

Daily Affirmation / Prayer / Inspirational Quote	Hours Slept

Excercise	Time Spent	Water	Daily Goals
		○ ○ ○ ○	
		○ ○ ○ ○	
		○ ○ ○ ○	

Nutritional Journal

	Nourishing Meals	Supplements/Essential Oils
BRKFST		
LNCH		
DNR		

Greens ○ Beans ○ Onions ○ Mushroom ○ Berries ○ Seeds ○

My Daily Planner

My Schedule for __/__/__

6:00 AM	
7:00 AM	
8:00 AM	
9:00 AM	
10:00 AM	
11:00 AM	
12:00 PM	
1:00 PM	
2:00 PM	
3:00 PM	
4:00 PM	
5:00 PM	
6:00 PM	
7:00 PM	
8:00 PM	
9:00 PM	
10:00 PM	
11:00 PM	
12:00 AM	

Daily Affirmation / Prayer / Inspirational Quote	Hours Slept

Excercise	Time Spent	Water	Daily Goals
		O O O O	
		O O O O	
		O O O O	

Nutritional Journal

	Nourishing Meals	Supplements/Essential Oils
BRKFST		
LNCH		
DNR		

Greens O Beans O Onions O Mushroom O Berries O Seeds O

My Daily Planner

My Schedule for __/__/__

6:00 AM	
7:00 AM	
8:00 AM	
9:00 AM	
10:00 AM	
11:00 AM	
12:00 PM	
1:00 PM	
2:00 PM	
3:00 PM	
4:00 PM	
5:00 PM	
6:00 PM	
7:00 PM	
8:00 PM	
9:00 PM	
10:00 PM	
11:00 PM	
12:00 AM	

Daily Affirmation / Prayer / Inspirational Quote	Hours Slept

Excercise	Time Spent	Water				Daily Goals
		O	O	O	O	
		O	O	O	O	
		O	O	O	O	

Nutritional Journal

	Nourishing Meals	Supplements/Essential Oils
BRKFST		
LNCH		
DNR		

Greens O Beans O Onions O Mushroom O Berries O Seeds O

My Daily Planner

My Schedule for __/__/__

6:00 AM	
7:00 AM	
8:00 AM	
9:00 AM	
10:00 AM	
11:00 AM	
12:00 PM	
1:00 PM	
2:00 PM	
3:00 PM	
4:00 PM	
5:00 PM	
6:00 PM	
7:00 PM	
8:00 PM	
9:00 PM	
10:00 PM	
11:00 PM	
12:00 AM	

Daily Affirmation / Prayer / Inspirational Quote	Hours Slept

Excercise	Time Spent	Water	Daily Goals
		○ ○ ○ ○	
		○ ○ ○ ○	
		○ ○ ○ ○	

Nutritional Journal

	Nourishing Meals	Supplements/Essential Oils
BRKFST		
LNCH		
DNR		

Greens ○ Beans ○ Onions ○ Mushroom ○ Berries ○ Seeds ○

My Daily Planner

My Schedule for __/__/__

6:00 AM	
7:00 AM	
8:00 AM	
9:00 AM	
10:00 AM	
11:00 AM	
12:00 PM	
1:00 PM	
2:00 PM	
3:00 PM	
4:00 PM	
5:00 PM	
6:00 PM	
7:00 PM	
8:00 PM	
9:00 PM	
10:00 PM	
11:00 PM	
12:00 AM	

Daily Affirmation / Prayer / Inspirational Quote	Hours Slept

Excercise	Time Spent	Water	Daily Goals
		O O O O	
		O O O O	
		O O O O	

Nutritional Journal		
	Nourishing Meals	Supplements/Essential Oils
BRKFST		
LNCH		
DNR		

Greens O Beans O Onions O Mushroom O Berries O Seeds O

My Monthly Planner

MONTH ______________________

Monday	Tuesday	Wednesday	Thursday

Healthy You Measurements					
Chest			Upper Arm		
Waist			Thigh		
Hips			Calf		

My Monthly Planner

MONTH ____________________

Friday	Saturday	Sunday	Special Notes

My Fitness Goals

My Weekly Planner

My Categories	Monday __/__/__	Tuesday __/__/__	Wednesday __/__/__

My Weekly Planner

Thursday __/__/__	Friday __/__/__	Saturday __/__/__	Sunday __/__/__

My Meal Planner

For Week of / /

	Breakfast	Lunch	Dinner	Groceries
Monday				
Tuesday				
Wednesday				
Thursday				
Friday				
Saturday				
Sunday				

Special Instructions and Notes

My Daily Planner

My Schedule for __/__/__

6:00 AM
7:00 AM
8:00 AM
9:00 AM
10:00 AM
11:00 AM
12:00 PM
1:00 PM
2:00 PM
3:00 PM
4:00 PM
5:00 PM
6:00 PM
7:00 PM
8:00 PM
9:00 PM
10:00 PM
11:00 PM
12:00 AM

Daily Affirmation / Prayer / Inspirational Quote	Hours Slept

Excercise	Time Spent	Water	Daily Goals
		○ ○ ○ ○	
		○ ○ ○ ○	
		○ ○ ○ ○	

Nutritional Journal

	Nourishing Meals	Supplements/Essential Oils
BRKFST		
LNCH		
DNR		

Greens ○ Beans ○ Onions ○ Mushroom ○ Berries ○ Seeds ○

My Daily Planner

My Schedule for __/__/__

6:00 AM	
7:00 AM	
8:00 AM	
9:00 AM	
10:00 AM	
11:00 AM	
12:00 PM	
1:00 PM	
2:00 PM	
3:00 PM	
4:00 PM	
5:00 PM	
6:00 PM	
7:00 PM	
8:00 PM	
9:00 PM	
10:00 PM	
11:00 PM	
12:00 AM	

Daily Affirmation / Prayer / Inspirational Quote	Hours Slept

Excercise	Time Spent	Water	Daily Goals
		○ ○ ○ ○	
		○ ○ ○ ○	
		○ ○ ○ ○	

Nutritional Journal

	Nourishing Meals	Supplements/Essential Oils
BRKFST		
LNCH		
DNR		

Greens ○ Beans ○ Onions ○ Mushroom ○ Berries ○ Seeds ○

My Daily Planner

My Schedule for __/__/__

6:00 AM	
7:00 AM	
8:00 AM	
9:00 AM	
10:00 AM	
11:00 AM	
12:00 PM	
1:00 PM	
2:00 PM	
3:00 PM	
4:00 PM	
5:00 PM	
6:00 PM	
7:00 PM	
8:00 PM	
9:00 PM	
10:00 PM	
11:00 PM	
12:00 AM	

Daily Affirmation / Prayer / Inspirational Quote	Hours Slept

Excercise	Time Spent	Water	Daily Goals
		○ ○ ○ ○	
		○ ○ ○ ○	
		○ ○ ○ ○	

Nutritional Journal

	Nourishing Meals	Supplements/Essential Oils
BRKFST		
LNCH		
DNR		

Greens ○ Beans ○ Onions ○ Mushroom ○ Berries ○ Seeds ○

My Daily Planner

My Schedule for __/__/__

6:00 AM
7:00 AM
8:00 AM
9:00 AM
10:00 AM
11:00 AM
12:00 PM
1:00 PM
2:00 PM
3:00 PM
4:00 PM
5:00 PM
6:00 PM
7:00 PM
8:00 PM
9:00 PM
10:00 PM
11:00 PM
12:00 AM

Daily Affirmation / Prayer / Inspirational Quote	Hours Slept

Excercise	Time Spent	Water	Daily Goals
		O O O O	
		O O O O	
		O O O O	

Nutritional Journal

	Nourishing Meals	Supplements/Essential Oils
BRKFST		
LNCH		
DNR		

Greens O Beans O Onions O Mushroom O Berries O Seeds O

My Daily Planner

My Schedule for __/__/__

6:00 AM	
7:00 AM	
8:00 AM	
9:00 AM	
10:00 AM	
11:00 AM	
12:00 PM	
1:00 PM	
2:00 PM	
3:00 PM	
4:00 PM	
5:00 PM	
6:00 PM	
7:00 PM	
8:00 PM	
9:00 PM	
10:00 PM	
11:00 PM	
12:00 AM	

Daily Affirmation / Prayer / Inspirational Quote	Hours Slept

Excercise	Time Spent	Water	Daily Goals
		○ ○ ○ ○	
		○ ○ ○ ○	
		○ ○ ○ ○	

Nutritional Journal

	Nourishing Meals	Supplements/Essential Oils
BRKFST		
LNCH		
DNR		

Greens ○ Beans ○ Onions ○ Mushroom ○ Berries ○ Seeds ○

My Daily Planner

My Schedule for __/__/__

6:00 AM	
7:00 AM	
8:00 AM	
9:00 AM	
10:00 AM	
11:00 AM	
12:00 PM	
1:00 PM	
2:00 PM	
3:00 PM	
4:00 PM	
5:00 PM	
6:00 PM	
7:00 PM	
8:00 PM	
9:00 PM	
10:00 PM	
11:00 PM	
12:00 AM	

Daily Affirmation / Prayer / Inspirational Quote	Hours Slept

Excercise	Time Spent	Water				Daily Goals
		○	○	○	○	
		○	○	○	○	
		○	○	○	○	

Nutritional Journal

	Nourishing Meals	Supplements/Essential Oils
BRKFST		
LNCH		
DNR		

Greens ○ Beans ○ Onions ○ Mushroom ○ Berries ○ Seeds ○

My Daily Planner

My Schedule for __/__/__

6:00 AM	
7:00 AM	
8:00 AM	
9:00 AM	
10:00 AM	
11:00 AM	
12:00 PM	
1:00 PM	
2:00 PM	
3:00 PM	
4:00 PM	
5:00 PM	
6:00 PM	
7:00 PM	
8:00 PM	
9:00 PM	
10:00 PM	
11:00 PM	
12:00 AM	

Daily Affirmation / Prayer / Inspirational Quote	Hours Slept

Excercise	Time Spent	Water	Daily Goals
		○ ○ ○ ○	
		○ ○ ○ ○	
		○ ○ ○ ○	

Nutritional Journal

	Nourishing Meals	Supplements/Essential Oils
BRKFST		
LNCH		
DNR		

Greens ○ Beans ○ Onions ○ Mushroom ○ Berries ○ Seeds ○

My Weekly Planner

My Categories	Monday __/__/__	Tuesday __/__/__	Wednesday __/__/__

My Weekly Planner

Thursday __/__/__	Friday __/__/__	Saturday __/__/__	Sunday __/__/__

My Meal Planner

For Week of / /

	Breakfast	Lunch	Dinner	Groceries
Monday				
Tuesday				
Wednesday				
Thursday				
Friday				
Saturday				
Sunday				

Special Instructions and Notes

My Daily Planner

My Schedule for __/__/__

6:00 AM	
7:00 AM	
8:00 AM	
9:00 AM	
10:00 AM	
11:00 AM	
12:00 PM	
1:00 PM	
2:00 PM	
3:00 PM	
4:00 PM	
5:00 PM	
6:00 PM	
7:00 PM	
8:00 PM	
9:00 PM	
10:00 PM	
11:00 PM	
12:00 AM	

Daily Affirmation / Prayer / Inspirational Quote	Hours Slept

Excercise	Time Spent	Water	Daily Goals
		O O O O	
		O O O O	
		O O O O	

Nutritional Journal

	Nourishing Meals	Supplements/Essential Oils
BRKFST		
LNCH		
DNR		

Greens O Beans O Onions O Mushroom O Berries O Seeds O

My Daily Planner

My Schedule for __/__/__

6:00 AM
7:00 AM
8:00 AM
9:00 AM
10:00 AM
11:00 AM
12:00 PM
1:00 PM
2:00 PM
3:00 PM
4:00 PM
5:00 PM
6:00 PM
7:00 PM
8:00 PM
9:00 PM
10:00 PM
11:00 PM
12:00 AM

Daily Affirmation / Prayer / Inspirational Quote	Hours Slept

Excercise	Time Spent	Water	Daily Goals
		○ ○ ○ ○	
		○ ○ ○ ○	
		○ ○ ○ ○	

Nutritional Journal

	Nourishing Meals	Supplements/Essential Oils
BRKFST		
LNCH		
DNR		

Greens ○ Beans ○ Onions ○ Mushroom ○ Berries ○ Seeds ○

My Daily Planner

My Schedule for __/__/__

6:00 AM	
7:00 AM	
8:00 AM	
9:00 AM	
10:00 AM	
11:00 AM	
12:00 PM	
1:00 PM	
2:00 PM	
3:00 PM	
4:00 PM	
5:00 PM	
6:00 PM	
7:00 PM	
8:00 PM	
9:00 PM	
10:00 PM	
11:00 PM	
12:00 AM	

Daily Affirmation / Prayer / Inspirational Quote	Hours Slept

Excercise	Time Spent	Water	Daily Goals
		○ ○ ○ ○	
		○ ○ ○ ○	
		○ ○ ○ ○	

Nutritional Journal

	Nourishing Meals	Supplements/Essential Oils
BRKFST		
LNCH		
DNR		

Greens ○ Beans ○ Onions ○ Mushroom ○ Berries ○ Seeds ○

My Daily Planner

My Schedule for __/__/__

6:00 AM	
7:00 AM	
8:00 AM	
9:00 AM	
10:00 AM	
11:00 AM	
12:00 PM	
1:00 PM	
2:00 PM	
3:00 PM	
4:00 PM	
5:00 PM	
6:00 PM	
7:00 PM	
8:00 PM	
9:00 PM	
10:00 PM	
11:00 PM	
12:00 AM	

Daily Affirmation / Prayer / Inspirational Quote	Hours Slept

Excercise	Time Spent	Water	Daily Goals
		○ ○ ○ ○	
		○ ○ ○ ○	
		○ ○ ○ ○	

Nutritional Journal

	Nourishing Meals	Supplements/Essential Oils
BRKFST		
LNCH		
DNR		

Greens ○ Beans ○ Onions ○ Mushroom ○ Berries ○ Seeds ○

My Daily Planner

My Schedule for __/__/__

6:00 AM
7:00 AM
8:00 AM
9:00 AM
10:00 AM
11:00 AM
12:00 PM
1:00 PM
2:00 PM
3:00 PM
4:00 PM
5:00 PM
6:00 PM
7:00 PM
8:00 PM
9:00 PM
10:00 PM
11:00 PM
12:00 AM

Daily Affirmation / Prayer / Inspirational Quote	Hours Slept

Excercise	Time Spent	Water	Daily Goals
		○ ○ ○ ○	
		○ ○ ○ ○	
		○ ○ ○ ○	

Nutritional Journal

	Nourishing Meals	Supplements/Essential Oils
BRKFST		
LNCH		
DNR		

Greens ○ Beans ○ Onions ○ Mushroom ○ Berries ○ Seeds ○

My Daily Planner

My Schedule for ___/___/___

6:00 AM
7:00 AM
8:00 AM
9:00 AM
10:00 AM
11:00 AM
12:00 PM
1:00 PM
2:00 PM
3:00 PM
4:00 PM
5:00 PM
6:00 PM
7:00 PM
8:00 PM
9:00 PM
10:00 PM
11:00 PM
12:00 AM

Daily Affirmation / Prayer / Inspirational Quote	Hours Slept

Excercise	Time Spent	Water	Daily Goals
		O O O O	
		O O O O	
		O O O O	

Nutritional Journal

	Nourishing Meals	Supplements/Essential Oils
BRKFST		
LNCH		
DNR		

Greens O Beans O Onions O Mushroom O Berries O Seeds O

My Daily Planner

My Schedule for __/__/__

6:00 AM	
7:00 AM	
8:00 AM	
9:00 AM	
10:00 AM	
11:00 AM	
12:00 PM	
1:00 PM	
2:00 PM	
3:00 PM	
4:00 PM	
5:00 PM	
6:00 PM	
7:00 PM	
8:00 PM	
9:00 PM	
10:00 PM	
11:00 PM	
12:00 AM	

Daily Affirmation / Prayer / Inspirational Quote	Hours Slept

Excercise	Time Spent	Water	Daily Goals
		○ ○ ○ ○	
		○ ○ ○ ○	
		○ ○ ○ ○	

Nutritional Journal

	Nourishing Meals	Supplements/Essential Oils
BRKFST		
LNCH		
DNR		

Greens ○ Beans ○ Onions ○ Mushroom ○ Berries ○ Seeds ○

My Weekly Planner

My Categories	Monday __/__/__	Tuesday __/__/__	Wednesday __/__/__

My Weekly Planner

Thursday __/__/__	Friday __/__/__	Saturday __/__/__	Sunday __/__/__

My Meal Planner

For Week of / /

	Breakfast	Lunch	Dinner	Groceries
Monday				
Tuesday				
Wednesday				
Thursday				
Friday				
Saturday				
Sunday				

Special Instructions and Notes

My Daily Planner

My Schedule for __/__/__

6:00 AM	
7:00 AM	
8:00 AM	
9:00 AM	
10:00 AM	
11:00 AM	
12:00 PM	
1:00 PM	
2:00 PM	
3:00 PM	
4:00 PM	
5:00 PM	
6:00 PM	
7:00 PM	
8:00 PM	
9:00 PM	
10:00 PM	
11:00 PM	
12:00 AM	

Daily Affirmation / Prayer / Inspirational Quote	Hours Slept

Excercise	Time Spent	Water	Daily Goals
		○ ○ ○ ○	
		○ ○ ○ ○	
		○ ○ ○ ○	

Nutritional Journal

	Nourishing Meals	Supplements/Essential Oils
BRKFST		
LNCH		
DNR		

Greens ○ Beans ○ Onions ○ Mushroom ○ Berries ○ Seeds ○

My Daily Planner

My Schedule for __/__/__

6:00 AM	
7:00 AM	
8:00 AM	
9:00 AM	
10:00 AM	
11:00 AM	
12:00 PM	
1:00 PM	
2:00 PM	
3:00 PM	
4:00 PM	
5:00 PM	
6:00 PM	
7:00 PM	
8:00 PM	
9:00 PM	
10:00 PM	
11:00 PM	
12:00 AM	

Daily Affirmation / Prayer / Inspirational Quote	Hours Slept

Excercise	Time Spent	Water	Daily Goals
		○ ○ ○ ○	
		○ ○ ○ ○	
		○ ○ ○ ○	

Nutritional Journal

	Nourishing Meals	Supplements/Essential Oils
BRKFST		
LNCH		
DNR		

Greens ○ Beans ○ Onions ○ Mushroom ○ Berries ○ Seeds ○

My Daily Planner

My Schedule for __/__/__

6:00 AM	
7:00 AM	
8:00 AM	
9:00 AM	
10:00 AM	
11:00 AM	
12:00 PM	
1:00 PM	
2:00 PM	
3:00 PM	
4:00 PM	
5:00 PM	
6:00 PM	
7:00 PM	
8:00 PM	
9:00 PM	
10:00 PM	
11:00 PM	
12:00 AM	

Daily Affirmation / Prayer / Inspirational Quote	Hours Slept

Excercise	Time Spent	Water	Daily Goals
		O O O O	
		O O O O	
		O O O O	

Nutritional Journal

	Nourishing Meals	Supplements/Essential Oils
BRKFST		
LNCH		
DNR		

Greens O Beans O Onions O Mushroom O Berries O Seeds O

My Daily Planner

My Schedule for __/__/__

6:00 AM	
7:00 AM	
8:00 AM	
9:00 AM	
10:00 AM	
11:00 AM	
12:00 PM	
1:00 PM	
2:00 PM	
3:00 PM	
4:00 PM	
5:00 PM	
6:00 PM	
7:00 PM	
8:00 PM	
9:00 PM	
10:00 PM	
11:00 PM	
12:00 AM	

Daily Affirmation / Prayer / Inspirational Quote	Hours Slept

Excercise	Time Spent	Water				Daily Goals
		O	O	O	O	
		O	O	O	O	
		O	O	O	O	

Nutritional Journal

	Nourishing Meals	Supplements/Essential Oils
BRKFST		
LNCH		
DNR		

Greens O Beans O Onions O Mushroom O Berries O Seeds O

My Daily Planner

My Schedule for __/__/__

6:00 AM	
7:00 AM	
8:00 AM	
9:00 AM	
10:00 AM	
11:00 AM	
12:00 PM	
1:00 PM	
2:00 PM	
3:00 PM	
4:00 PM	
5:00 PM	
6:00 PM	
7:00 PM	
8:00 PM	
9:00 PM	
10:00 PM	
11:00 PM	
12:00 AM	

Daily Affirmation / Prayer / Inspirational Quote	Hours Slept

Excercise	Time Spent	Water	Daily Goals
		O O O O	
		O O O O	
		O O O O	

Nutritional Journal

	Nourishing Meals	Supplements/Essential Oils
BRKFST		
LNCH		
DNR		

Greens O Beans O Onions O Mushroom O Berries O Seeds O

My Daily Planner

My Schedule for __/__/__

6:00 AM
7:00 AM
8:00 AM
9:00 AM
10:00 AM
11:00 AM
12:00 PM
1:00 PM
2:00 PM
3:00 PM
4:00 PM
5:00 PM
6:00 PM
7:00 PM
8:00 PM
9:00 PM
10:00 PM
11:00 PM
12:00 AM

Daily Affirmation / Prayer / Inspirational Quote	Hours Slept

Excercise	Time Spent	Water	Daily Goals
		○ ○ ○ ○	
		○ ○ ○ ○	
		○ ○ ○ ○	

Nutritional Journal

	Nourishing Meals	Supplements/Essential Oils
BRKFST		
LNCH		
DNR		

Greens ○ Beans ○ Onions ○ Mushroom ○ Berries ○ Seeds ○

My Daily Planner

My Schedule for __/__/__

6:00 AM	
7:00 AM	
8:00 AM	
9:00 AM	
10:00 AM	
11:00 AM	
12:00 PM	
1:00 PM	
2:00 PM	
3:00 PM	
4:00 PM	
5:00 PM	
6:00 PM	
7:00 PM	
8:00 PM	
9:00 PM	
10:00 PM	
11:00 PM	
12:00 AM	

Daily Affirmation / Prayer / Inspirational Quote	Hours Slept

Excercise	Time Spent	Water	Daily Goals
		○ ○ ○ ○	
		○ ○ ○ ○	
		○ ○ ○ ○	

Nutritional Journal

	Nourishing Meals	Supplements/Essential Oils
BRKFST		
LNCH		
DNR		

Greens ○ Beans ○ Onions ○ Mushroom ○ Berries ○ Seeds ○

My Weekly Planner

My Categories	Monday __/__/__	Tuesday __/__/__	Wednesday __/__/__

My Weekly Planner

Thursday __/__/__	Friday __/__/__	Saturday __/__/__	Sunday __/__/__

My Meal Planner

For Week of / /

	Breakfast	Lunch	Dinner	Groceries
Monday				
Tuesday				
Wednesday				
Thursday				
Friday				
Saturday				
Sunday				

Special Instructions and Notes

My Daily Planner

My Schedule for __/__/__

6:00 AM
7:00 AM
8:00 AM
9:00 AM
10:00 AM
11:00 AM
12:00 PM
1:00 PM
2:00 PM
3:00 PM
4:00 PM
5:00 PM
6:00 PM
7:00 PM
8:00 PM
9:00 PM
10:00 PM
11:00 PM
12:00 AM

Daily Affirmation / Prayer / Inspirational Quote	Hours Slept

Excercise	Time Spent	Water	Daily Goals
		○ ○ ○ ○	
		○ ○ ○ ○	
		○ ○ ○ ○	

Nutritional Journal

	Nourishing Meals	Supplements/Essential Oils
BRKFST		
LNCH		
DNR		

Greens ○ Beans ○ Onions ○ Mushroom ○ Berries ○ Seeds ○

My Daily Planner

My Schedule for __/__/__

6:00 AM	
7:00 AM	
8:00 AM	
9:00 AM	
10:00 AM	
11:00 AM	
12:00 PM	
1:00 PM	
2:00 PM	
3:00 PM	
4:00 PM	
5:00 PM	
6:00 PM	
7:00 PM	
8:00 PM	
9:00 PM	
10:00 PM	
11:00 PM	
12:00 AM	

Daily Affirmation / Prayer / Inspirational Quote	Hours Slept

Excercise	Time Spent	Water	Daily Goals
		○ ○ ○ ○	
		○ ○ ○ ○	
		○ ○ ○ ○	

Nutritional Journal		
	Nourishing Meals	Supplements/Essential Oils
BRKFST		
LNCH		
DNR		

Greens ○ Beans ○ Onions ○ Mushroom ○ Berries ○ Seeds ○

My Daily Planner

My Schedule for __/__/__

6:00 AM	
7:00 AM	
8:00 AM	
9:00 AM	
10:00 AM	
11:00 AM	
12:00 PM	
1:00 PM	
2:00 PM	
3:00 PM	
4:00 PM	
5:00 PM	
6:00 PM	
7:00 PM	
8:00 PM	
9:00 PM	
10:00 PM	
11:00 PM	
12:00 AM	

Daily Affirmation / Prayer / Inspirational Quote	Hours Slept

Excercise	Time Spent	Water	Daily Goals
		O O O O	
		O O O O	
		O O O O	

Nutritional Journal

	Nourishing Meals	Supplements/Essential Oils
BRKFST		
LNCH		
DNR		

Greens O Beans O Onions O Mushroom O Berries O Seeds O

My Daily Planner

My Schedule for __/__/__

6:00 AM
7:00 AM
8:00 AM
9:00 AM
10:00 AM
11:00 AM
12:00 PM
1:00 PM
2:00 PM
3:00 PM
4:00 PM
5:00 PM
6:00 PM
7:00 PM
8:00 PM
9:00 PM
10:00 PM
11:00 PM
12:00 AM

Daily Affirmation / Prayer / Inspirational Quote	Hours Slept

Excercise	Time Spent	Water	Daily Goals
		O O O O	
		O O O O	
		O O O O	

Nutritional Journal		
	Nourishing Meals	Supplements/Essential Oils
BRKFST		
LNCH		
DNR		

Greens O Beans O Onions O Mushroom O Berries O Seeds O

My Daily Planner

My Schedule for __/__/__

6:00 AM	
7:00 AM	
8:00 AM	
9:00 AM	
10:00 AM	
11:00 AM	
12:00 PM	
1:00 PM	
2:00 PM	
3:00 PM	
4:00 PM	
5:00 PM	
6:00 PM	
7:00 PM	
8:00 PM	
9:00 PM	
10:00 PM	
11:00 PM	
12:00 AM	

Daily Affirmation / Prayer / Inspirational Quote	Hours Slept

Excercise	Time Spent	Water	Daily Goals
		○ ○ ○ ○	
		○ ○ ○ ○	
		○ ○ ○ ○	

Nutritional Journal		
	Nourishing Meals	Supplements/Essential Oils
BRKFST		
LNCH		
DNR		

Greens ○ Beans ○ Onions ○ Mushroom ○ Berries ○ Seeds ○

My Daily Planner

My Schedule for __/__/__

6:00 AM	
7:00 AM	
8:00 AM	
9:00 AM	
10:00 AM	
11:00 AM	
12:00 PM	
1:00 PM	
2:00 PM	
3:00 PM	
4:00 PM	
5:00 PM	
6:00 PM	
7:00 PM	
8:00 PM	
9:00 PM	
10:00 PM	
11:00 PM	
12:00 AM	

Daily Affirmation / Prayer / Inspirational Quote	Hours Slept

Excercise	Time Spent

Water			
O	O	O	O
O	O	O	O
O	O	O	O

Daily Goals

Nutritional Journal

	Nourishing Meals	Supplements/Essential Oils
BRKFST		
LNCH		
DNR		

Greens O Beans O Onions O Mushroom O Berries O Seeds O

My Daily Planner

My Schedule for __/__/__

6:00 AM	
7:00 AM	
8:00 AM	
9:00 AM	
10:00 AM	
11:00 AM	
12:00 PM	
1:00 PM	
2:00 PM	
3:00 PM	
4:00 PM	
5:00 PM	
6:00 PM	
7:00 PM	
8:00 PM	
9:00 PM	
10:00 PM	
11:00 PM	
12:00 AM	

Daily Affirmation / Prayer / Inspirational Quote	Hours Slept

Excercise	Time Spent	Water	Daily Goals
		O O O O	
		O O O O	
		O O O O	

Nutritional Journal

	Nourishing Meals	Supplements/Essential Oils
BRKFST		
LNCH		
DNR		

Greens O Beans O Onions O Mushroom O Berries O Seeds O

My Weekly Planner

My Categories	Monday __/__/__	Tuesday __/__/__	Wednesday __/__/__

My Weekly Planner

Thursday __/__/__	Friday __/__/__	Saturday __/__/__	Sunday __/__/__

My Meal Planner

For Week of / /

	Breakfast	Lunch	Dinner	Groceries
Monday				
Tuesday				
Wednesday				
Thursday				
Friday				
Saturday				
Sunday				

Special Instructions and Notes

My Daily Planner

My Schedule for __/__/__

6:00 AM
7:00 AM
8:00 AM
9:00 AM
10:00 AM
11:00 AM
12:00 PM
1:00 PM
2:00 PM
3:00 PM
4:00 PM
5:00 PM
6:00 PM
7:00 PM
8:00 PM
9:00 PM
10:00 PM
11:00 PM
12:00 AM

Daily Affirmation / Prayer / Inspirational Quote	Hours Slept

Excercise	Time Spent	Water	Daily Goals
		○ ○ ○ ○	
		○ ○ ○ ○	
		○ ○ ○ ○	

Nutritional Journal

	Nourishing Meals	Supplements/Essential Oils
BRKFST		
LNCH		
DNR		

Greens ○ Beans ○ Onions ○ Mushroom ○ Berries ○ Seeds ○

My Daily Planner

My Schedule for __/__/__

6:00 AM	
7:00 AM	
8:00 AM	
9:00 AM	
10:00 AM	
11:00 AM	
12:00 PM	
1:00 PM	
2:00 PM	
3:00 PM	
4:00 PM	
5:00 PM	
6:00 PM	
7:00 PM	
8:00 PM	
9:00 PM	
10:00 PM	
11:00 PM	
12:00 AM	

Daily Affirmation / Prayer / Inspirational Quote	Hours Slept

Excercise	Time Spent	Water	Daily Goals
		○ ○ ○ ○	
		○ ○ ○ ○	
		○ ○ ○ ○	

Nutritional Journal

	Nourishing Meals	Supplements/Essential Oils
BRKFST		
LNCH		
DNR		

Greens ○ Beans ○ Onions ○ Mushroom ○ Berries ○ Seeds ○

My Daily Planner

My Schedule for __/__/__

6:00 AM	
7:00 AM	
8:00 AM	
9:00 AM	
10:00 AM	
11:00 AM	
12:00 PM	
1:00 PM	
2:00 PM	
3:00 PM	
4:00 PM	
5:00 PM	
6:00 PM	
7:00 PM	
8:00 PM	
9:00 PM	
10:00 PM	
11:00 PM	
12:00 AM	

Daily Affirmation / Prayer / Inspirational Quote	Hours Slept

Excercise	Time Spent

Water			
O	O	O	O
O	O	O	O
O	O	O	O

Daily Goals

Nutritional Journal

	Nourishing Meals	Supplements/Essential Oils
BRKFST		
LNCH		
DNR		

Greens O Beans O Onions O Mushroom O Berries O Seeds O

My Daily Planner

My Schedule for __/__/__

6:00 AM	
7:00 AM	
8:00 AM	
9:00 AM	
10:00 AM	
11:00 AM	
12:00 PM	
1:00 PM	
2:00 PM	
3:00 PM	
4:00 PM	
5:00 PM	
6:00 PM	
7:00 PM	
8:00 PM	
9:00 PM	
10:00 PM	
11:00 PM	
12:00 AM	

Daily Affirmation / Prayer / Inspirational Quote	Hours Slept

Excercise	Time Spent	Water	Daily Goals
		○ ○ ○ ○	
		○ ○ ○ ○	
		○ ○ ○ ○	

Nutritional Journal

	Nourishing Meals	Supplements/Essential Oils
BRKFST		
LNCH		
DNR		

Greens ○ Beans ○ Onions ○ Mushroom ○ Berries ○ Seeds ○

My Daily Planner

My Schedule for __/__/__

6:00 AM	
7:00 AM	
8:00 AM	
9:00 AM	
10:00 AM	
11:00 AM	
12:00 PM	
1:00 PM	
2:00 PM	
3:00 PM	
4:00 PM	
5:00 PM	
6:00 PM	
7:00 PM	
8:00 PM	
9:00 PM	
10:00 PM	
11:00 PM	
12:00 AM	

Daily Affirmation / Prayer / Inspirational Quote	Hours Slept

Excercise	Time Spent	Water	Daily Goals
		O O O O	
		O O O O	
		O O O O	

Nutritional Journal

	Nourishing Meals	Supplements/Essential Oils
BRKFST		
LNCH		
DNR		

Greens O Beans O Onions O Mushroom O Berries O Seeds O

My Daily Planner

My Schedule for __/__/__

6:00 AM	
7:00 AM	
8:00 AM	
9:00 AM	
10:00 AM	
11:00 AM	
12:00 PM	
1:00 PM	
2:00 PM	
3:00 PM	
4:00 PM	
5:00 PM	
6:00 PM	
7:00 PM	
8:00 PM	
9:00 PM	
10:00 PM	
11:00 PM	
12:00 AM	

Daily Affirmation / Prayer / Inspirational Quote	Hours Slept

Excercise	Time Spent	Water	Daily Goals
		○ ○ ○ ○	
		○ ○ ○ ○	
		○ ○ ○ ○	

Nutritional Journal

	Nourishing Meals	Supplements/Essential Oils
BRKFST		
LNCH		
DNR		

Greens ○ Beans ○ Onions ○ Mushroom ○ Berries ○ Seeds ○

My Daily Planner

My Schedule for __/__/__

6:00 AM	
7:00 AM	
8:00 AM	
9:00 AM	
10:00 AM	
11:00 AM	
12:00 PM	
1:00 PM	
2:00 PM	
3:00 PM	
4:00 PM	
5:00 PM	
6:00 PM	
7:00 PM	
8:00 PM	
9:00 PM	
10:00 PM	
11:00 PM	
12:00 AM	

Daily Affirmation / Prayer / Inspirational Quote	Hours Slept

Excercise	Time Spent	Water	Daily Goals
		O O O O	
		O O O O	
		O O O O	

Nutritional Journal		
	Nourishing Meals	Supplements/Essential Oils
BRKFST		
LNCH		
DNR		

Greens O Beans O Onions O Mushroom O Berries O Seeds O

What's the Next Step?

THANK YOU for purchasing, reading and your support!

I hope you have enjoyed learning how to transform your health and business while protecting and nurturing your NUMBER ONE asset in your business...YOU!

Now that you have your system of step-by-step instructions to transform your health and business, it is time for you to practice using the Essential Tools to improve your mindset, become better organized, and take better care of your health.

Use the *Visionary Solution System* to keep your motivation alive and stay focused on what you want. Regularly update your strategic action plan template to get to the next step of your goal. Start networking with your *Circle of Five* to keep you inspired.
Use the Vision Board Success Secrets to give legs to your dreams.

If you desire more, here are some of my **Success School** online programs.

Transformational 30 Day Challenge:

- *Healthy You Toolbox*
- *Healthy Business Toolbox*
- *Author Toolbox*

Success School Club Mentor Membership

If you are still overwhelmed with how to prioritize your goals, or don't even know where to begin, you might benefit from business visionary sessions.
SOLOpreneurs are isolated and don't have others with which to bounce off.
They don't have anyone who truly understands the pressures and challenges of being a SOLOpreneur.

Some of the finest sports figures in the world still have a training coach. The individual talent is there, and the coach's role is to help hone those skills to achieve maximum potential. A business visionary session is no different, and my **Success School** online mentor membership will help to maximize the performance of your business "muscles."

Success School helps fast-track your success and avoid the school of hard knocks through an online, step-by-step transformational learning experience.

Thank you for purchasing the **Action Attraction ™ Planner**

The **Action Attraction Planner** is a 90 Day Transformational Health & Wealth Planner. This is a great complementary workbook tool to use while applying the skills that you learned in the *Healthy Business, Healthy You Toolbox* Book.

This Health & Business Tool can help your WISHES and Goals come true.

Let me help you take the Next Step.

THANK YOU Gift for YOU.
Please use the coupon code below to access the
30 Day Transformational challenge for $97 (Value $297).

Transformational 30 Day Challenge

This 30 day program has taught many people from varied backgrounds how to achieve any goal using a simple step by step process. In 30 days you can achieve any goal with the right focus and guidance. Laura provides this guidance and motivation and will show you how to go from "wishing" to "doing" by taking action in only 30 days.

You will also read real-life success stories from clients who have followed the *30 Day Transformational Challenge* program. They will share how they applied this system to improve their lives, enhance their businesses, achieve author goals, and overcome health challenges. Did you know that you're 95% more likely to accomplish your goals if you have a community to support you?

Join now and get started down the road to success in everything you do. Making your dreams into reality is only a few clicks away.

- Private VIP Facebook Group Community
- Share your Vision Board in our group room
- Access to Online Learning Center

Sign up at: https://LivewithLaura.com/30days

Gift for you!
$200 Off

Enter code:
200OFFAAPVIP

(Reminder coupon code is in capital letters)

Connect with Laura Cole Gonzalez

Facebook www.facebook.com/LiveWithLaura

Twitter www.twitter.com/LiveWithLaura

Instagram www.instagram.com/livewithlaura/

Pinterest www.pinterest.com/livewithlaura/

YouTube www.youtube.com/LivewithLauraTV

Periscope http://www.Periscope.tv/livewithlaura

Website www.livewithlaura.com/

Healthy Business, Healthy You Toolbox Book

Action Attraction Planner

To Order or Reorder **Action Attraction Planner**

https://livewithlaura.com/actionattractionplanner

I WISH you Health, Wealth and Happiness with Grace and Ease!

Laura